GHOSTS ON
THE COAST
OF MAINE

GHOSTS ON
THE COAST
OF MAINE

By
Carol Olivieri Schulte

Illustrations by Jo Going

Down East Books

ISBN 978-0-89272-390-4

Cover art by Anita Crane
Original text design by Dick Nixon

Down East Books
www.nbnbooks.com

Library of Congress Cataloging-in-Publication Data

Schulte, Carol Olivieri, 1947–
    Ghosts on the coast of Maine / by Carol Olivieri Schulte.
       p.   cm.
    ISBN 0-89272-390-4 (pbk.)
    1. Ghosts–Maine. 2. Haunted places–Maine 3. Maine–History.
  I. Title
  BF1472.U6S34   1996
  133.1'09741–dc20   96-7900
                                 CIP

CONTENTS

PREFACE

This book is about ghosts. All of the stories are based in fact, but some names were changed to protect the identities of those who actually experienced these happenings.

I thank all the people who generously allowed me to be a part of their lives during my summer's research on the coast of Maine. They shared their families, their secret thoughts, and their dearly held memories. I will not forget them.

Carol Olivieri Schulte

A Note About the Illustrations

Jo Going illustrated *Ghosts on the Coast of Maine,* bringing to the book her experience as children's book illustrator for Houghton Mifflin Publishing Company and art director for *Boston Now* magazine.

Her work has been exhibited at Harvard University; Siegel Contemporary Art, New York City; and Anton Gallery, Washington, D.C.; as well as Maine Coast Graphics in Camden, Maine; and the Root Cellar Gallery in Rockland, Maine.

(8)

CHAPTER ONE

THE BENNETT BOY

ld-timers don't much like talkin' about it. A glint of fear and then annoyance escapes through their seawater eyes whenever a "tourist" broaches the subject. The way these lobstermen figure, if something bad happens to somebody it's because he deserved it. It's also a matter between that person and His Maker, so it's nobody else's business.

Only a person who'd grown up in Port Clyde every summer of her life would get to hear the whole Bennett story. That's why I lucked out.

Carl Bennett was a hard-working man in the early 1900s. Every lobsterman was. Out haulin' from 4 A.M. till 2 P.M., when your catch got weighed, made for long days. When you weren't haulin' or settin' traps, you were fixin' your nets or lettin' your skiff swell up so she'd quit leakin'.

He was a good deal fonder of his lobster boat than he was of his wife, Cora. Everybody knew this because Carl did not follow the Maine custom of naming his boat after his wife.

Carl came from a high-strung Scandinavian line. He liked things his way, and he liked them his way here and now. He tried to control his temper, but more often than not, it got the better of him. His face would redden underneath that almost white thatch of hair, and he'd bellow so loud the natives of the neighboring island could hear him. He wasn't a drinking man, but when he got mad he lashed out at anything—the kitchen dishes, the living room lamp, Cora's favorite vase. Sometimes even Cora became injured in the fracas.

Cora put up with him long enough to bear him two blond, handsome sons. Ben, the youngest, was Carl's favorite. Carl took him everywhere he went. He taught him how to row a dory, how to make traps, bait them, set them, and haul them. On bad weather days, Carl and Ben could often be found painting buoys or tarring unraveled rope in Carl's little lobster shack. In summer they'd catch flounder off the wharf with hand lines made by Carl. In the colder months they'd go deer hunting around by Turkey Cove. Carl put all the love and affection he didn't give to his wife and older son into his relationship with Ben.

Cora saw her sons grow till the youngest was twelve. Then she jumped off the town wharf one night and ended her torturous life.

Ben took it hard. He quit paying attention in school and got into a lot of fights. When school was out for the summer, his dad had a hard time getting him up mornings to help lobster so they could have food on the table. Ben turned to his companions for friendship, but they were not the kind of people he needed. His friends would steal cigarettes and then go on ventures that kept them out all night long. They were always looking for trouble.

One night, during the full swing of Prohibition, they found it. There had been stories of rumrunners on the coastal islands, but no one thought they'd ever come into port. These outlaws were reported to be ruthless in their endeavors, tough men who'd shoot you dead rather than ask questions.

Ben and his friends were walking down the lighthouse road, cigarettes in hand, when one of the boys thought he spotted the light of a ship through the thick pine trees. They crept closer to shore to investigate. Sure enough, a bunch of strange men were unloading huge kegs onto the rocky shore just in front of the lighthouse. They were strong and dangerously armed.

What happened next is hard to say. Either the boys made a noise, or the tips of their lit cigarettes betrayed their presence. In any case, the rum-runners chased after the boys and caught up with one of them, Ben. With blade held high, an outlaw severed Ben's head in one blow. The other boys got away.

The ruffians threw the remnants of Ben's body in a swamp off the lighthouse road. Realizing that they were in danger of a potential attack by towns-people, they loaded the kegs back on board and continued their nocturnal journey.

Carl was beside himself with grief when he

learned of the violent death, and he lived out the rest of his days a heartbroken man.

About twenty years after Ben's death, a man was walking down the lighthouse road with his wife and daughter. The little girl turned to see a man following them. He was described as heavy set with dark hair and beard, old-fashioned clothes and high black boots. The little girl started to run, and the man ran after her, brandishing a huge knife. Her parents turned around and they too became alarmed, scooped up their daughter, and ran full speed ahead. After several yards they checked back, and saw only the tall pine trees behind them. The menacing figure had disappeared. When they came to their senses, they realized that the "man's" boots had made no sound on the road.

Since then, several townspeople have reported seeing a huge, gruff-looking man with a knife chasing after a blond youth, down by the lighthouse. The sighting was reported being in the area of the swamp that lined the road just before the lighthouse.

Ten years ago, people on four separate occasions witnessed a big man with a blade chasing after them. The faster they'd run, the faster he'd run, until he vaporized into nothingness. Again, no sound of running footsteps was noticed.

Others have seen only the figure of a light-haired boy standing above the swamp water by the lighthouse.

Either one or both of the figures were reportedly being seen up until about five years ago.

"Tourists" still seem to have an immense fascination with the lighthouse road. The townspeople have tried to discourage them by erecting a sign that says "Dead End." It certainly was, many years ago, for a boy named Ben.

(14)

CHAPTER TWO

JEWELL'S BOUTIQUE

ewell Stone is her real name. This sapphire-eyed lady, once my Maine neighbor, carries her name well because she is a gem of a person. Those star-bright eyes harbor a sense of playful daring and hilarious laughter, but there is a no-nonsense side to Jewell that has made her the successful businesswoman that she is today. This is why, when she told me her place in Rockland was haunted, I had no trouble believing her story.

This dainty, well-coiffed effervescence of femininity described what happened one day when she was minding the store. At that time, 1979, the store was loaded with antiques, costume clothing, and secondhand articles. It was not the plushily carpeted house of high fashion that it is now. The floorboards were bare, and there was more of a funky, offbeat atmosphere to the place. Purses decorated with moons and stars hung in the doorway instead of big bright leather bags with silver clips. The aroma of incense tingled the nose.

One day in broad daylight, when Jewell was alone in the store, she heard the distinct sound of booted footsteps in the next room. When she walked over to investigate, she found no person. She did notice that a pair of Civil War boots on display amid some antiques had moved from one end of the room to the other. It gave her goose bumps, and it still gives her goose bumps to talk about it.

Jewell summoned her courage and continued to relate more curious happenings. She told me that within the first five minutes of being in the place, before she bought it, she knew that there was a ghost about. This statement was interesting, because a bed-and-breakfast proprietress in another Maine town had told me the same thing about her establishment, two days before. I asked Jewell what she thought of her first ghostly impression. She said that she put it in the back of her mind because she had too many other things to think about at the time, starting a new business and turning the house into a store.

Her impression could not be forced to stay in the back of her mind, however, the day she turned on a light which was immediately turned off by someone not visible to the physical eye. Later on, a door shut that had just been opened. No wind, no cause, no person. For no apparent reason, she started calling him George. Every time an article was moved out of place, it was "George's" doing.

I sensed a military presence in the house, based

on the connection with the war boots, but I wasn't sure which war. Jewell said that anything was possible, since her place had been a funeral home prior to her ownership, but she didn't know exactly when.

"Funeral home" started buzzing around in my mind after I left my gutsy neighbor. (Jewell was the first person to give written consent to use her name and that of her establishment, in this book.) "Vietnam War Era" came to mind next, and that's all I knew until I talked to the former operator of the funeral home.

Dewey wasn't sure he wanted to talk to me. I suppose my non-Maine accent made him wary. Figuring this, I gradually slipped into my best "ay-uh" kind of speech, and we had ourselves a grand old chat. As it turned out, Dewey knew my family because last fall he had taken care of my grandmother's body before her Providence undertaker could make the 365-mile journey up here. That put us on even better terms.

Come to find out, there had been a young chap from Rockland about twenty-seven years old, whose body had been flown in from Hawaii. Dewey didn't rightly know which year, either 1967 or 1968. The fellow had quite a nice service, as he recalled, an outdoor military funeral on a beautiful day in May, with guns smokin' and practically the whole town out to mourn him. He had died in a car accident in Hawaii while stationed there in the army. His name: George Golden.

His widow was quite shook up about it. She was just a young thing, no kids or anything. She ran a small ice cream shop on the outskirts of town, that is, until George died. Then she took up and moved away, and nobody's seen her since. There was reason for her to be upset, as well as the whole town, actually.

George had sort of been their fair-haired boy. He was an all-star basketball, football, and track athlete. Many a time he had put his high school on the front page of the newspaper. After George graduated, he continued lobster fishing with his father, a decorated veteran of World War II. Their whole family was very patriotic.

When George signed up for the army, he was determined to make himself a hero. Ayuh. He was going to fight them Commies, yes sir, the finest kind of fighter there'd be. He'd put his hometown on the map, by God. George Golden, from Rockland, Maine.

And then his life got cut short. George wasn't a wild one; he was in the passenger seat of the car when it happened. One of his army buddies got drunk and drove the two of them right smack into a tree. There he was, halfway to Vietnam, but he never made it.

Dewey wanted to know why I thought the Golden fellow was the ghost. I explained to him about my "feelings" with regard to the presence in the house, and why George would make a perfect ghost. A violent death is a prime factor, since the spirit is jolted from the physical sphere to the non-physical sphere. The soul may be confused, may not understand that its body is dead. Secondly, George's death would have been a huge frustration

(18)

to him. He didn't want to die in some silly accident, he wanted to go out in triumphant glory, fighting for his country. He had anticipated a more honorable death, one with an enemy bullet lodged in his chest or something. That's why he's been bugging Jewell for attention. He'd like to relay this emotional burden to someone in hopes of being relieved of it.

All I can say is, George, you did your best. Let it go at that.

CHAPTER THREE

HAUNTED MOUNTAIN

arah Whitesell was surrounded by her loving family when she died. This cushion of strength and goodwill allowed her to pass on gracefully, without much confusion, but her spirit has remained here as a testament of youthful innocence and gentility. Even if you cannot see her, her presence unmistakably permeates the last bit of ground her feet trod upon, the Mt. Megunticook trail.

Her life story was short but meaningful for those around her. It was full of energy and sensitivity toward others. It ended May 6, 1865, two days after her thirteenth birthday.

On that day the Whitesell family decided to go "Maying," in celebration of a crisp, sunny Lincolnville morning. They hitched up the buggy and rode west, discussing which place was best for a picnic.

Father Whitesell didn't have much to say. He was too busy driving the buggy. Sarah and her two little brothers were arguing about their favorite spots, so Mother had to play arbitrator. The boys wanted to go to the shore because they loved to play in the water, and they didn't want to spend time climbing up a mountain. Sarah kept talking about the mountain because she liked to skip through the leafy passages of light where birds sang to one another in the treetops. It was so pretty, and there were interesting rocks and flowers to collect all along the way.

Mother hesitated to interrupt long enough for Father to intervene. "We'll go to the mountain," he said.

Sarah hugged her father. He was so strong and kind and mostly gave in to her when there was a choice to be made. Zachariah Whitesell felt close to his daughter, the family member most interested in the profession he had chosen, the practice of law. Even though she did not understand everything she read down at his office, she loved to keep her father company, poring over the dusty old books full of big words. As with her father, criminal cases were her favorite.

Mary Whitesell shrugged her shoulders in acquiescence. She wasn't about to take on daughter and husband at the same time, both strong-willed personalities. She gave Sarah a knowing glance, however, because she knew that her daughter would be concerned about her feelings. Mary then settled down the boys, and they were all off to Mt. Megunticook in the Camden hills.

The air was so clean and the sun so bright that they caught Sarah's spirit from the beginning of the trail. She bounced up the path like a mountain goat, checking back now and then to make sure that her little brothers were not too far behind. She wanted this to be a pleasant trip for them, since it had been her idea.

By the time they reached the top, Mary had grown tired so she sat down in the soft long grass. Sarah went over and rubbed her mother's shoulders, then proceeded to help her father spread the blanket and take food out of the picnic basket. "Wouldn't it make a nice touch to have some flowers with our spread," she thought. The most colorful blooms were growing about twenty feet away, on the edge of the precipice. Sarah picked some, then turned around to show her mother. At that point a gust of wind knocked her off balance, and she tumbled off the thousand-foot cliff onto a rocky shelf several hundred feet below.

Zachariah was first to reach her, after much difficulty. There lay her form, small for thirteen years of age, unbroken but unconscious. Now it looked even smaller, unmoving, helpless, and extremely bruised. The little girl's condition paralleled her father's feelings.

It took a while to gather rescue team members, but they did their best, lashing her to a plank and lowering her from crag to crag. It was a painstaking operation that lasted several hours. Sarah was brought to the nearest house, where everything possible was done to save her life. She passed away that evening, however.

Sarah's family, along with the family in the house, knelt down at her body and prayed through most of the night. They wanted her to be as happy now, as she had made them during her lifetime. The next morning Zachariah talked with Mary about erecting some sort of memorial on Sarah's mountain at the spot where she had slipped. A white wooden cross was decided upon and placed on the small hill overlooking the cliff.

Many people have traveled the path up Mt. Megunticook since then. It's a long walk, but it is so beautiful that a sense of purification captures the soul. The higher altitude might produce some lightheadedness, but that's to be expected. One might be tempted to walk over to the edge of the mountaintop and catch sight of the whole expanse of Lake Megunticook and miles of surrounding lands below. Be careful, especially when the wind is blowing.

It is the wind that blends with the spirit of Sarah and enfolds a person standing on top of the mountain. It bends the gentle grass backward and turns one's head ever so slightly in the direction of the tall weather-beaten cross several feet away. It creates a chilling effect that might be heightened by the sight of a little girl hovering in the flowers with an angelic smile on her face.

According to one witness, Sarah wears the clothes of her era, and colors can be distinguished, although her form is translucent. Another woman, a teacher, relates that Sarah does not stay long, and only seems to appear in the spring and summer months. People have experienced her as a non-threatening presence, simply a warm glow of friendliness. The sightings have been on good weather days, not cloudy or foggy ones, and the frequency of Sarah's visits was greatest during the 1930s and early '40s. The last reported appearance was in 1976.

Sarah's flowers might be tempting, too, but the locals warn not to pick anything atop that mountain. They consider it bad luck. They want to keep Sarah's mountaintop a place of inspiration and light, a place that people will remember by name, "Maiden's Cliff."

(26)

CHAPTER FOUR

THE COASTER MAKER

he lucrative shipping era of 1864–1874 produced men with big personalities and derring-do. They were generous with their investments (they could afford to, no income tax), then turned around and socked most of their money into supporting the home town.

Shipbuilding was the industry that allowed most of these men to live out their dreams, but it was also a risk because it dealt with the sea. These men didn't mind the challenge; they welcomed it. Because ship merchants were not afraid to put their money to good use, small coastal towns boomed with business.

Tenants Harbor was the best example of this. Every other dock was littered with loads of cargo headed for Boston; New York; or Savannah, Georgia. They were boarded on schooners called coasters, which were built in the shipyards of Tenants Harbor. The busiest shipyard was Armstrong & Keane.

Gilbert Armstrong fit the description of a nineteenth-century shipping magnate. He was proud, healthy and bold. He loved to look out upon the harbor and see piles of lumber, coal, and stone, waiting to be loaded on the queenly coaster ships that belonged to him. In the other direction, toward town, he could see the general store that he owned, which was a good-sized contribution to the Tenants Harbor economy.

Gilbert stuck to the commercial end of the shipping industry. A shrewd trader, he knew ships, shipmasters, and buying and selling of materials. He was the richest and most respected merchant in town. He had a good eye for quality, and that's what he saw just west of his establishment, in the year 1872.

Harry Keane, ship builder, had just moved to Tenants Harbor and had set up shop on the shore below Armstrong. Harry was an excellent craftsman, with much experience and ability to choose the best materials for the job. He worked alone, but when the product was finished, she was a first-rate ship.

Harry was also a good talker. When he realized the success of Armstrong's operation, he coupled that with his own artistry as a builder, and asked his neighbor to go into business with him. Together they would build the most, the finest, the lowest-priced vessels of any shipyard on the coast.

In 1873 Armstrong agreed. The two partners successfully complemented one another. What Keane lacked in business sense was demonstrated by Armstrong; when Gilbert had a question about what wood to use, Harry supplied the answer.

Their common denominator was guts. A large part of their business was shipping paving blocks, a rather heavy cargo, literally the cornerstones of Fifth Avenue buildings, before concrete came along. Armstrong & Keane soon added lime to their list of shipped products, which was risky because of its propensity to catch fire when wet.

Seven strong vessels were launched out of the Armstrong & Keane shipyard. All were lost at sea. Nature was the one factor that Gilbert and Harry had not been able to predict.

Also difficult to foresee was the faster pace of the world and the invention of steamers, then railroads, and today's trucks. The age of the great three-masted sailing vessels began to wane in 1874.

In that year stood the unfinished frame of the eighth coaster at Armstrong & Keane. Construction had been halted by a workmen's strike and consequent lawsuits. The shipyard was forced to pay salaries by the company-store method. This broke the company. Armstrong & Keane dissolved. Harry moved to Camden to work in another yard, and Gilbert concentrated on running his store.

Financial blows seem to be part of the human condition, but Gilbert took this one personally. He felt that he had disappointed the town as well as his family. He didn't feel too kindly toward Harry at first, because his partner had deserted him for greener pastures, but as time passed, he simply missed the deep friendship that had highlighted their working relationship.

The world had taken Armstrong by surprise and given him a whirl. He never came out of it. Once a sturdy and upright gentleman, he lived out his last days a thin and worried man, burdened by guilt and loneliness.

Over the years, all the buildings of the Tenants Harbor shipyard have been transformed. The big white shoreline building became an inn.

The East Wind Inn houses a ghost who has been seen climbing the main staircase, wending his way to the window overlooking the sea. He stops to gaze out across the waters that once harbored the likes of his grand fleet of ships.

He manifests himself in several ways. The owner of the inn, who lives in the basement apartment, awoke one night to the sound of footsteps and the swinging doors that squeak upon entrance to the dining room. When the proprietor went to investigate, the only thing he noticed was the doors still swinging.

An older middle-aged woman who had been a friend of the owner's for quite some time and a faithful guest, eagerly called him on the interhouse phone one evening. "Tim, you'd better come up and take a look at this."

He went up to the second floor to see what was the matter. There was glass all over the floor. "Jenny," he said, "didn't you remove the stick that was under the window when you tried to shut it?"

"Tim," she replied, "I never touched the window."

Jenny then moved to another room. A couple of days later, Tim received another phone call. This time broken glass was scattered all over the room. It looked as though something had smashed through the window from the outside. This, of course, would have been impossible, because the storm window remained securely in place.

The winter of 1987 a woman doctor and her husband were staying in one of the rooms on the third floor overlooking the ocean. She felt a sudden chill while in bed, so she decided to get up and get an extra blanket. She found that she couldn't move. There was a pressure on her body that was holding her flat on the bed. The woman told the presence, "Please go, this is making me very uncomfortable. I can't deal with this right now."

The pressure eased. In the morning she said to Tim, "So who's the ghost?"

The unfortunate soul that had been trying to break through his dimensional barrier in one way or another was someone who needed sympathy and understanding. He was the product of an unfinished journey. It was Gilbert Armstrong in a different time, a different place.

CHAPTER FIVE

THE HOUSE OF HEALING

n the little town of Thomaston, I locked horns with a man who denounced my ghostly delvings. It was a friendly fight, nobody got hurt, but it was revealing. He stood talking to me with arms folded like a granite statue, while he berated me for pursuing what he considered the Devil's playground. There are no ghosts because we have no consciousness when we are dead, he argued. We are "as if asleep," he quoted from the Bible.

The man had given me a great frame of reference. "As if asleep" closely defines my concept of ghosts. Upon entering the dream state, we experience a level of awareness that is quite different from our everyday consciousness. It might seem confusing or disconnected, but we deal with it in such a way that it helps us work out our problems or anxieties.

Ghosts are spirits in a dream world. They are

not at their final destination. Some need help in getting there; others have already been there and have returned to help us. Also, by their manifestations they are reminders of the spiritual world, so often forgotten in this strongly materialistic society of ours.

The ghost in the "House of Healing" is a returnee. He is present in a house built in 1830, a time of much unsettlement in the northern New England world. New Englanders were still recovering from fighting the English one last time, and they were on unsure ground with the surrounding Indians. Eighteen thirty was only seven years prior to the Atticus the Slave incident involving Thomaston, a typical prelude to the Civil War Era.

Walter James had to survive in this kind of environment when he was alive. He had to keep the optimism of his fellow townspeople at a high level, so that they would not be disturbed by the uncontrollable forces around them. Walter's job, as he saw it, was to soothe nerves and try to preserve peace.

He accomplished this by throwing himself into as many town projects as he could. His energy level was high, but it was expressed in a modest, reticent way. Walter wasn't one to boast about his achievements. Maybe for that reason today's Thomastonians do not speak much about what he accomplished, which, upon inspection, seems to be a great deal.

James built not only his own house, but many others as well. He was a person of business interests who bought and sold real estate. He was one of the founders of the Thomaston Bank, established an insurance company, and saw to it that the stately grove of elms that now lines Main Street was planted and maintained. Walter was the driving force behind the library, the school, and a church of his choice.

Adults were not the only ones to benefit from his magnanimous personality. Walter, who remained childless, kept a swing in his stable barn for the neighborhood children. Many a Saturday afternoon he'd spend pushing kids on the swing or teaching them the basic skills of woodworking, his favorite pastime. The barn was Walter's place.

Just ask the two male photography students who resided in the loft of that barn during the winter of 1986. They weren't exactly frightened and were never harmed, but they always felt that someone was watching them. Their cat appreciated the presence a little more than the boys. When the boys moved to another room in the house, the cat continued to live in the barn that has basically remained untouched since its construction.

Another student, Virginia, who took a room in the winter of 1987, had no doubt about the presence of a ghost in the house. She came downstairs one morning to find a pair of candles still on the mantelpiece, but the candlesticks neatly placed on the floor below.

Ginny was witness to other happenings that involved Betty, the present owner of the house. Betty was laid up with a broken foot, which restricted her to a wheelchair. She had a cane, but that was only for very short distances.

One particular evening a storm was brewing. A person who had grown to hate storms from her Texas days, Betty sat in the living room worrying about the upstairs windows that were open. Her dog, Penny, who snarled at any intruder or threatening creature, was calmly keeping her company by the fireplace. All of a sudden Betty heard the windows slam upstairs. The dog never peeped. Shortly afterwards Ginny, the only tenant at the time, rushed in the door and hurried up the stairs. She came down just as quickly. "Did you walk up those stairs to close the windows?" she scolded. Betty said, "No. 'Somebody else' did it for me."

That "somebody else" must have been watching one night when Virginia locked the front door. Betty was with her, instructing her how to shut it, because it sticks. She saw Ginny lock the door. About 6:30 the next morning, as Betty walked down the stairs, she intuitively knew that the door was unlocked, even though it was still closed. She tried it. Sure enough, it was unlocked. When Ginny came down, Betty asked if she had been out earlier that morning. Virginia said, "No, I just woke up."

To get back to my original statement about Walter, how does he help those who have lived in his house? Throughout the years Walter has exuded a relaxing, welcoming feeling of warmth that creates a healthy state of mind for the occupants. Great stress therapy. One foot in the door can tell you that.

He has especially carried out his tradition in his "choice" of owners. Since 1899, a most hospitable boardinghouse operator and three doctors have lived in and performed their occupational functions in his house. Many people today still talk about all the times they or their children or families were healed in that wonderful old place. One thing's for sure, an inhabitant would never be lonely.

(38)

CHAPTER SIX

BURNT HEAD

uicide is a whole other trip. It produces the most bizarre and sometimes the most dangerous effects of any kind of ghost.

Because of their deliberate choice to cut short their progression of spiritual growth, these souls are at the lowest stage of light beyond the material world. They are frustrated, they are regretful, and they are trying to make up for their mistake, but they need assistance. Their desperation makes for intense manifestations. They cannot harm you, but they might come close.

Cathlin Warren did not realize any of this on Monhegan Island in June 1962. She did not believe or disbelieve in ghosts, and she had never given the matter much thought during her twenty-two-year lifetime.

Twenty-six years later, Cathlin is a successful professor of art at a prominent university, and enjoys much respect and popularity in her area as an artist-in-residence. Every once in a while she still ponders her Monhegan happening. It is only because I am not using her real name that I can in good conscience repeat what she had to tell me.

This young girl of Irish descent was the daughter of two show business people. Her father was a saxophone player in a New York studio band, and her mother was a former Broadway dancer who operated her own dance studio in the city. Her dad was never home, so her childhood memories are mostly of her mother, Peg.

Peggy Warren started to act differently when Cathlin was about twelve. She became very quiet and withdrew into herself. Her large blue eyes turned a dull gray, with darkened patches of skin underneath. Her mouth, so contoured for laughter, never smiled. Sometimes it was difficult for her to acknowledge her daughter when Cathlin was speaking to her. Other times, Peg never responded at all.

One August Cathlin noticed that her mother had worn long-sleeved leotards to class all summer long. Later on she found out that it was to hide the razor-blade scars. Those horrible purplish marks did not belong on such slender, artistic arms, but they never went away, especially in Cathlin's mind.

Mrs. Warren did not perish from the self-inflicted wounds. She did become institutionalized, however, and finally died, leaving her daughter pretty much on her own. Cathlin's path seemed to lean towards the arts, so she chose painting.

In 1962 Cathlin was doing well as an artist one

year out of college. The money situation was decent, she had a steady boyfriend whom she liked well enough, and she was pleased with her art work. For some inexplicable reason, she had started to dive into a deep depression. In an attempt to shake herself out of it, Cathlin had packed up her paints and headed for Monhegan Island. For years this out-to-sea island had provided the Warren family with wholesome, refreshing vacations. It was a natural choice.

Cathy was not prepared for what would happen next. The second evening of her stay at one of the older inns on the island, she decided to take a walk. With nothing particular in mind, Cathy meandered towards town. She soon found herself on the trail to Burnt Head, one of the cliff heads located on the back of the island, facing the open ocean.

It was a humid, muggy evening, but any walk on Monhegan at any time is such a visual uplift that Cathy continued over the rocky road lined with wild roses and trailing yew. No one else was around when she passed through the trees onto the bare ledges of Burnt Head. There was no wind.

As Cathlin stood looking out over the sea, she felt herself being pushed towards the edge of the cliff by a pair of hands on her shoulders . . . step by step, slowly but perceptibly. Cathy turned to see who it was, but there was no one behind her. She started to run back toward town, but she was halted. Again the "hands" pushed her to within a three-foot distance from the edge of the cliff. "This is it," Cathy thought. "I'm going to be pushed over the edge of the cliff by this invisible entity. No one will know what happened, and I'll never get a chance to explain."

The "hands" stopped, but relief was not in sight. Cathy's feet remained planted, but something overtook her feelings and sensations. All at once she was mentally falling through the air, out of control. Her body became numb, followed by a huge force of pain surging through her brain, traveling all the way down her spine, legs, arms. The broken body that had dashed itself on the rocks was now filling with fluid, filling and filling. There was a terrific tightening in the lungs which pushed up to the head and burst there.

This took place in a matter of seconds. Then a distinctly female presence cried, "Help," and departed.

Cathy was too overwhelmed to be afraid. She walked back to town thinking, "I can't tell anyone any part of this. No one will believe me. I will have to keep this one to myself. Besides," she chuckled, "they'd start putting me away before I'd even get halfway through the explanation."

She did not sleep well that night. The next day Cathlin tried to sort it all out and came to the conclusion that she would have to find out the meaning of what had happened to her before she could be at peace. At least now she was out of her depression. That much had been accomplished.

Between the libraries and local historians, Cathy discovered that one evening back in 1947 an eighty-year-old woman, living alone above the wharf gift shop, had jumped off Burnt Head and drowned. She had taken her cat to shore, had it put to sleep, settled her financial affairs, and come back to the island. Unbeknownst to anyone, she had walked the path to the cliff and ended her life. Her body was found the next day.

Did Cathy relive the experience of the unfortunate elderly lady? Was Cathy chosen to receive this information because the young artist could have empathized, and thereby helped relieve the lady?

Or was it some sort of warning from her own mother?

CHAPTER SEVEN

BANK ACCOUNT BREAKER

This house had come to my attention through four Maine residents who claimed it to be haunted, one of whom traveled with me to point out the location. Upon entering South Thomaston, I noticed a spot where a small bridge functioned as the belt between two larger bodies of water, known as the Gig. Around the bend, coming north on Route 73, we came upon a huge block of a house the color of creamed coffee. Its hip-roofed structure dwarfed the neighboring dwellings, some of which were older than the Victorian house in question. There was definitely something about the top of that house that drew my attention. It was not female.

No one was living in the house, so we peeked in the windows that were not sheeted over. The original velvet drapes framed what seemed like an age-old scene from an antique doll house. Wooden carvings of grape clusters studded the stocky legs

(45)

of a low, wide piano, which stood in front of a conversation grouping of a brocaded settee and chairs. Keeping watch over the piano was the tall, slender sentinel of a lamp. It was topped with colored glass sections of a tulip-shaped shade. As we turned to continue walking, a sharp odor of fire hit my nostrils. Looking around and seeing nothing amiss, I quickly dismissed the sensation.

A room on the east side seemed like a lighthouse unto itself, with an ornate brass table lamp dominating a small area that jutted out from the rest of the house. It was this room that smelled of the sea, with old charts on the walls that hung opposite black-framed photographs of schooner ships. A sea captain's reading room, for sure.

Although these furnishings were of great value, the house itself looked sorely neglected. The walls were crumbling, the majestic front door was weather-beaten, and the barn attached to the house was leaning on the main structure for support. Above the barn door was a sign spelling out the exact name of the school I had attended for twelve years, and that omen spurred me on to research the place.

The local historian lived several miles down the road, so off we went. He said that a sea captain had built the mansion in 1855, the year after a fire had destroyed his first house constructed on the same plot of ground. This comment triggered my memory about the odor I had encountered. After perusing photographs and old records, we asked about the present owner and found a parallel between his circumstances and the captain's.

Ghosts will do this. They will often choose to communicate to a person or inhabitant who has been through a predicament similar to theirs. This situation allows for a sympathetic ear, on both sides of the line.

First, the captain's story: Josiah Thurston, in spite of his rural elementary education, went on to pursue an intellectual career. The Honorable Thurston practiced law for a while until he became interested in business. Then he reverted to family tradition and chose a marine occupation, operating a shipyard on the Wessaweskeag. Translation from the Indian is Tidal Creek Place, nicknamed "The Gig." Within eighteen years, he had built nineteen vessels.

Josiah adjusted well. During the first seven years of marriage, which were childless, he spent most of his time bolstering his law and ship-building businesses. When the children came, he worked even harder to keep his family well fed and able to continue in the lifestyle to which they were accustomed.

In 1848 this father of a growing brood was elected a Selectman of Thomaston, a job which he took very seriously. He was appointed to a committee which traveled to Augusta, and his law training served him well in the devising of bills and in lobbying the State Legislature for passage of them. Shortly afterwards he became a state senator.

The 1854 fire dismayed but did not discourage Thurston. Politics was in his blood by this time, and he decided to go for it. He was going to build the biggest, most elegant mansion in the Knox/ Waldo County area, including a ballroom on the floor above the barn. It would serve as a good family home, but oh, would it impress his ever-growing list of Washington friends and cronies.

Ambition became reality. By 1860 Josiah was rubbing noses with the likes of Hannibal Hamlin, the vice presidential running mate of Abraham Lincoln. Thurston's single-handed campaign to swing Knox County for the Hamlin/Lincoln ticket was so impressive that the new President invited him to consider a high Washington office.

The Civil War intervened, and Lincoln's offer was disregarded. After a brief stint in Cassius Clay's Battalion, Thurston returned home in 1861 to find that he was a man deep in debt. Politics had kept him from being on top of the shipyard's finances, and it had also inspired him to borrow lavish sums for the construction and decoration of his house.

Determined to keep his "dream house," Josiah switched gears and assumed a new career, that of sea captain. In one winter he absorbed all the books on navigation that were available to him, then took command of a ship the following spring. It was a valiant effort but not quite sufficient to bail him out of his money troubles. His brother made him a deal, which rendered the unfinished mansion to the brother. Josiah moved to another town and remained a sea captain as long as his physical constitution permitted.

Just as Josiah's highest aspiration was all wrapped up in his mansion, so was Avery Henderson's. Avery, the present owner, a man of books and letters and local politics, tackled the business of buying the Thurston house in 1986. He told everyone of his restoration plans and how much he wanted the place to be beautiful again.

Avery was enthralled with the new purchase. He tried to raise money for the restoration by having huge lawn sales. He dragged valuables from his Massachusetts home and sold them on the lawn of the mansion. He tried for two years.

During those years, he knew that he and his family were not alone in the house. While he'd be busy in his workroom, he'd hear footsteps on the floor above. His wife heard a knock on the front door once and opened it to vacant space. After one of his lawn sales, when everything was put away and in order, Avery looked up to the semi-dark sky to see the figure of a man in seafaring clothes watching him from the roof. Two others saw it; then it disappeared. The "man" seemed to be concerned about the outcome of the sale. Would it be enough to help the owner make a go of it?

The third year Avery realized that his attempts had failed. The house was just too expensive to finish and restore. The neighbors hardly ever saw his Massachusetts car in the driveway. That is why we were able to look into the windows and catch a glimpse of a ghostly past, along with the ghostly present.

CHAPTER EIGHT

PITCHER MAN

Maine coast towns were perfect targets for British depredation during the Revolutionary War, and Goose River was no exception. The town took its name from the high-banked stream that flows over chunky green-mossed rocks to become part of the great harbor. Across the river spanned a small wooden bridge, the significance of which will be revealed in the course of this chapter.

The British took it upon themselves to pester the inhabitants of Goose River, notwithstanding the hardy temperament of these early Americans. They would sail down the coast in vessels called "shaving mills" and disembark to steal cattle, butter, or guns. Sometimes they made women and children take to the woods while they burned their houses.

The husbands of these women fought back with everything they had, ambushing the invaders from the woods or volleying shots from the shoreline shrubbery. There were no soldiers assigned to protect this little town, so the settlers had to be ingenious. One fellow, upon sight of a British barge, ran for his drum and started to beat "roll call," while another fellow shouted military commands to an imaginary band of troops. The barge passed on.

The patriot from Goose River who gained the most recognition during this time was a fisherman named William Richardson. Bill happened to be at the right place at the right time for his greatest act of valor. It was 1779 and Revolutionary sentiment was at fever pitch, especially aboard the privateer of Commodore Samuel Tucker. This ambitious American captain spied an English East Indiaman bound for the coast of Maine, loaded with a bountiful cargo of East Indian goods. He captured the ship, stole the cargo, and was heading toward Goose River when he realized that he was unfamiliar with the area and needed guidance. Meanwhile another English ship had been alerted to Tucker's deed and was in hot pursuit of the miscreant.

The bright eye of Captain Tucker rested upon a small fishing boat and he drew up to it at once. He immediately enlisted the services of the pilot, William Richardson, and together they journeyed about sixty miles up to Harpswell. Here they anchored by the ledges and remained out of the enemy's reach, since the British vessel was much larger and could not come close to shore. This did not deter the English captain, who blockaded the port and was awaiting reinforcements.

Tucker feared for his ship, but Richardson told him to hold on until the first storm. It was then that the American ship, guided by the skillful hands of the Goose River navigator, slipped past the enemy in the thick black of night. Driven by the northeast wind, she sailed on to Portland.

The British captain was not aware of the escape till morning, at which time he hightailed it west. Richardson had done his job well, however, and only allowed the enemy a fleeting glimpse of the Yankee privateer rounding the bend at Cape Elizabeth. She had passed the point of being overtaken and safely continued on to her destination, Salem, Massachusetts.

Richardson was pleased to have avenged his townspeople for the plunderings they had suffered at British hands. By the war's end, Goose River residents had endured their crops being burned, their animals slaughtered, and their houses razed. That is why, when these people learned of the Treaty of Paris in 1783, they gathered for the biggest, wildest party ever thrown in the area. It was, of course, hosted by William Richardson.

It began with a burst of cannon shot booming its echo throughout the Penobscot mountains. Guns were fired and drums beat in order to call the neighboring citizens of Camden and Castine. Civilians, soldiers, and officers poured in from the garrisons of Penobscot Bay to celebrate the long-awaited victory.

Pitchers of ale and canisters of tobacco adorned all the tables and sideboards of Bill's house. Not an inch of space was bare. A pig was killed for the feast, as well as a lamb and a steer. Fifers blew on their high-pitched instruments for a circle of dancing men wielding drink mugs, while others roared patriotic war songs. It was a wondrous evening of revelry that went far into the night.

At one point during the celebration, after several mugs of ale, Bill decided to go wandering about town with a pitcher full of brew, rousting out anyone who was missing the party. He went ambling down the road, singing and yelling, peering in any window with a light in it, and knocking on those with none. The road took him down the hill from his house and over to the bridge across the river. There he met three horsemen, to whom he jubilantly offered his pitcher of ale. Not realizing that they were Tories, who were suffering enough indignation on this eventful day, Bill never gave a thought to any malice. As he held out his pitcher, one of the men struck him in the head with the butt of his gun and rendered him unconscious. The three travelers sped off and left Bill to die, never knowing what hit him.

The bridge has since been replaced, and the town renamed Rockport, but it is still the haunt of William Richardson. Nineteen twenty is the earliest anyone can remember hearing about the Revolutionary War hero who stalks the bridge with a pitcher in his hand.

One night in the late summer of 1953, a young couple was approaching the bridge, when the girl grabbed onto her boyfriend in rigid fear. At the other end of the bridge was a man coming towards them, holding something out in front of him. He seemed purposeful. The boyfriend prepared to defend his female companion against the weird stranger, when suddenly the man disappeared. After they had calmed down, they realized that what they had seen was no ordinary personage.

The area around the bridge is significant also. It is a cozy glen, suitable for lovers. About ten years after the latter incident, two couples were parked in this quaint, wooded spot. They were too busy having fun to notice a man approaching from the rear. One of the guys rolled down a window to get some air and in so doing came face to face with a man holding a pitcher towards him. The guy quickly rolled up the window and told the driver to step on the gas.

Old-timers chuckle whenever they hear one of the Rockport lovers' lane stories. They know better than to go meandering around there after dark. They attend to the sign, "No trespassing between sunset and sunrise."

(56)

CHAPTER NINE

WRECK ISLAND

Nobody would go up with me to Wreck Island, formerly False Franklin, four miles southwest of Friendship Harbor. 'Course I'd just told 'em that I'd read it was haunted (maybe that had something to do with it). On the other hand, any place with a name like that sounded dangerous for any craft, so I left our fifteen-foot Glassmaster at her mooring and gassed up the Buick for the trip.

It was a long one. Going up and down roller coaster hills on narrow two-lane roads with low visibility and lack of signs made a stomach-stressed journey. I was well rewarded, however, when I took a wrong turn and drove up the drive-way of Eaton Stearns. Ol' Eaton came out (I'd never seen him before in my life) and said, "By Gawd, I hope you're looking for me."

I hesitated, then laughed, "Well I don't rightly know. Can you tell me about Wreck Island?"

(57)

He said, "No, but I can take you there. Do you trust me?"

I said, "For the time bein'."

Eaton and I went down the road some, till he stopped at a small beach on Martin's Point. "There she is," he pointed out.

We got in a green punt that badly needed paint, and rowed out far enough for me to get a good look at the island. It was such a pretty sight with the sun beaming down on her beige rocks and the air so still around her. In clear daylight it was hard to imagine what devastation had been wreaked by this little spot of sunshine in the sea.

Stan Bushman, an old fisherman laid up with the gout, tells the story. December 4, 1768, was the date. The ship *Winnebec,* sailing from Boston, got caught in a storm and lost control around the ledges of False Franklin. The cold wind and driving snow was some fierce, and it blasted that boat against the rocks and stove her to pieces.

Early the next morning supposedly, some fishermen on their way out to sea found some boards on Cranberry Island, some debris on Harbor Island, and then the wreck on False Franklin. Eleven bodies of crew and passengers were sprawled out on the shore.

The men left their fishing and went ashore to see if anyone was alive. Seeing none, they loaded chests full of valuables, clothes, and provisions aboard their boats. It took them about seven trips to do this, and they weren't noticed by anyone till they were about done. When it was learned that the *Winnebec* had washed up on the island, several townspeople went out to investigate, and proceeded to notify the authorities.

Meanwhile, by the time of that seventh trip, a terrible squall had blown up, bringing with it violent torrents of ice and snow. The fishermen could not make it back to the mainland, so they had to stay on False Franklin overnight. What happened to them that night was something they never wished to experience again.

Since the island was uninhabited, the men sought out branches large enough to make a lean-to. Between the branches and the boards from the wreck, they devised a shelter with a floor and bedded down for the night. The snow had stopped, but it was bitter cold.

A few hours past them sleeping, a breeze found its way into the shelter and stirred Alan Page, one of the men. He woke up and started choking and gagging; he could not catch his breath. His partially frozen eyelids finally opened up to see a "man" with clothes drenched, leaning over him, clutching Alan's throat with his hands. Alan gasped, then no sound came from his throat. The sleeper next to him shook Page and brought him to, whereupon this second fisherman also felt a constriction around his throat. The whole camp was invaded by figures outlined in white light, intent on giving the men a taste of what it felt like to be strangled.

"Now my father," Stanley said as he drew on his pipe, "always told me that he'd heard that them fishermen had murdered the people off of that ship. O' course, he'd fished those waters many times himself, and he claimed that one night he and Georgy Green started out toward Franklin. The moon was exceptionally bright, and they looked over to see some shapes roaming around in a cloud of light. They got no closer, but they'd never forget that sight."

Stanley admitted that he's seen lights hovering over the island on occasion. A friend of his was passing by the island shortly after evening had set in, once, and saw what looked like the hull of a ship half buried in the sand. He'd never seen anything there before, so he went over to take a look. By the time he'd reached the spot, it was gone.

On my way back from Friendship, I was mulling over Wreck Island, and skepticism about the possibility of murder came to mind. Why would a group of fishermen, minding their own business, kill some poor shipwrecked people over some food and supplies? My thoughts continued.

The mishap occurred in the middle of a northern winter. Cold, snow, and ice make land transportation difficult, if not impossible, for an out-of-the-way place like a peninsular village. The roads (?) could easily get blocked with snow, so that neither man nor horse could pass. These ideas came to me as I maneuvered one of the difficult "s" curves peculiar to the Maine backwoods.

The weather would have rendered fishing vessels useless at least part of the season, while making sea transportation dangerous and oftentimes fatal. The year 1768 did not know lighthouses, channel markers or marine patrol of any kind. Great quantities of food and medicine would have been hard to come by. If an opportunity arose to gather goods like woolen blankets or dried meats, a man would think of his family first, and consequences last.

Besides, the unfortunate seagoers were probably half dead by the time they were discovered. Between fighting ocean waves, getting dashed on the rocks, and being exposed to low temperatures, they must have been spent. A strong twist of rope around the neck would have easily finished them. I'm not saying the "murders" should be condoned, but circumstances do make that version of the story more plausible. Murder would also have been motivation for the simulated strangulations.

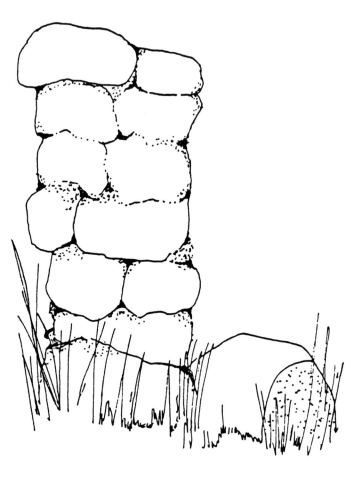

(62)

CHAPTER TEN

THE INVISIBLE ESTATE

raveling up Route One, one would come across a town nestled in the deep woods atop a hill going down to the ocean. It is a town of surprises, especially about evening. The trees that line the narrow roads of Northport are so thick that they form clusters of forest around the houses. Even going slowly in a car, one is startled by the appearance of these narrow, high-roofed dwellings that seem to pop out of nowhere.

Most of these houses belong to the eighteenth or nineteenth century, with little odd-shaped windows and peculiar wood carvings decorating the eaves. One of them is shared by three old women, whose portrait bears a marked resemblance to the females that spun the fates of mankind in Greek mythology. Nevertheless, they are all kind enough to share their knowledge about an event that occurred in their town the night of December 16, 1954.

It was a night full of Christmas cheer and eager anticipation at the home of Mr. and Mrs. Edward Cosgrove. This affluent couple had inherited the family real estate business, enabling them to indulge in all the luxuries of the day: two Cadillacs, a Rolls-Royce, a greenhouse of exotic plants, and a private golf course. These were the trimmings of a magnificent estate furnished with the finest quality furniture and items throughout.

The Cosgroves were even lucky enough to secure two intelligent and loving people to watch over their children and the house whenever they were gone. Mr. and Mrs. Walden adored the Cosgrove boys, aged five, seven, and nine, and treated them like grandchildren. They knew how to be strict, though, when necessary. The youngest one was forever leaving his toys about, setting up potential booby traps for unsuspecting passersby. Mrs. Walden patiently trained him to pick up after himself. It was Mrs. Walden who had told her employers of the creative playthings she had seen in a Boston store catalog.

That was why that night Mr. and Mrs. Cosgrove were on their way to Boston on a shopping spree for the children. They had softened the blow of their departure by choosing that day to decorate the whole mansion, inside and out. They had put up the tallest and fullest Christmas tree they could find. Colored lights illuminated trees, bushes, the outside of the house, and a special Santa Claus display on the roof.

The three little boys were not in a mood for early bedtime, so Mr. and Mrs. Walden read the boys' favorite stories until they nodded off to sleep. The substitute grandparents lifted the children out of their slumbering positions into their beds and retired themselves. That was the last peaceful moment in the lives of these five people.

An hour later found them choking and gasping for air, as they battled the smoke and flames of a fire that ripped through the large house and crumbled it to the ground. It left nothing but two chimneys, some badly warped household appliances, and a set of iron lawn chairs and table.

Firemen and neighbors fought the blaze for hours, saving the house next door, but they were too late to do anything about the two adults and their young charges. The charred remains of Mrs. Walden and the children lay in the southeastern corner of the foundation with those of Mr. Walden twenty feet away. Mr. and Mrs. Cosgrove came home to a graveyard instead of a holiday house. They could only stare in mute grief at the sole remnant of their little boys' world: a toy sailboat resting unharmed, on the iron table.

No one knew the cause of the fire. It could have been the furnace or could have been a faulty electrical system. What everyone did realize was that money isn't everything. A wonderful life of comforts and riches had been reduced to ashes in a matter of minutes.

The saddened parents moved away, and the land passed on to a multimillionaire from Chicago, and then to a Texas oil man who married a local girl. Neither party built over the location of the catastrophe. They both left the stubble of a chimney standing in a field of its own and constructed tennis courts and other buildings up the hill from it.

The "Three Fates" look over their coffee cups and caution to beware of the site. They say that Brent Severson, a well-respected farmer, was walking along the road by that place one night and heard some little kids screaming their lungs out. There was a light in the trailer across the road, but nothing extraordinary was going on. The house across from it seemed to have nothing going on either, and they were the only two homes around that had any kids. Severson looked over to that field and saw that half a chimney just sitting there growing weeds around it, and he decided to walk briskly the rest of the way home.

Cal Owens, a town preacher, was known to have been walking by the place with his two daughters, when they all heard crying and screaming of small children. They knelt down right there in the road and prayed a bit. Then they went home to tell Mrs. Owens.

Another time a family was visiting the area on vacation. It was a cloudy day, no day for the beach, so the parents left their kids to play in the town park. The husband and wife got their camera out of the car and started walking up the hill, towards the Cosgrove estate road. The stone chimney ruins caught their eye, and they took several snapshots of the area.

A week later they got their pictures back, and instead of the photos of an old chimney, there were the pictures of a huge white mansion with two chimneys, all intact. The couple figured that the developing studio had mixed up their pictures with someone else's, and checked it out. No, there had been no mistake. There were also no photos of a lone chimney.

Within the last three years there have been so many incidents of people taking pictures of a "house that wasn't there," that Northport has become famous for its unusual haunted house. There's even a photograph hanging on the wall of the local diner. You can hardly get more significant than that.

(68)

CHAPTER ELEVEN

TAUKOLEXIS

ou won't see him in the middle of the day, when tourists are winding their way around the tower after paying their dollar at the desk. The visitors are curious about the old iron artifacts, the muskets, the view from the top. The children point out the cannon balls and try to move an extra large one attached to a podium. They all pass him by. No one thinks to prowl around the huge jagged boulder lightly veiled in the damp shade of the foundation. It is here that his spirit lurks, to remind us of the pain endured in imprisonment.

Taukolexis came to be a prisoner in Fort William Henry, at Pemaquid, by doing a friend a favor. The date was February 1696. Chiefs Egremet, Toxus, and Abenaquid had stopped at Taukolexis's camp to seek company for a peacemaking journey to Fort William Henry. They noticed a tall, stalwart man squatting by a fire and asked him to come along. The man looked at them with strong eyes and told them that he would be unafraid to go, but that his wife and children were sick and needed his care. There was another man, equally as able as he and compassionate enough to take his place on the trip, his friend and neighbor.

So it was that Taukolexis went with the three chiefs to see if a prisoner exchange could be worked out with Captain Crabb, commander of the fort. The men stopped at another Indian camp and gained several recruits before arriving at their destination, white flag in hand. Considering all the recent fighting that had occurred between the French and Indians and the English settlers at Pemaquid, everyone knew that the operation, though well-intended, would be risky.

Fort William Henry was such a bone of contention because it was of great importance to all parties. The Indians wanted it free and clear for transportation. They wanted to be able to paddle their canoes around that point, instead of the treacherous Pemaquid Point farther out on the ocean. During English occupancy, they were forced to use Pemaquid Point, today a beautiful spot graced by a grand lighthouse. Back then, however, the mass of rocks and spirited seas surrounding the Point were not marked by any sort of warning.

The French, who most of the time convinced the Indians to team up with them, wanted the fort because the English had it. And the English wanted it because they thought they deserved any spot of ground that they landed on.

Being a man grounded in English philosophy, Captain Crabb was not about to let an opportunity for domination go by. In the midst of the treaty negotiations, the captain and his men attacked the Indians, killing Egremet, Abenaquid, and two others. Toxus and a few followers escaped, while Taukolexis was taken prisoner at the garrison.

Many months passed. It was a terrible winter for the captive Indian. He was not used to being chained to a wall, in a dark space with not much food. He was a child of the forest, a wanderer of the land. No man had ever captured him like an unsuspecting animal in a trap. His soul longed for clean air and warmth of the sunshine. He could hear the soothing roll of the ocean waves, but he could not bathe his body or taste the healing salt of the sea.

Once in a while in early spring, the soldiers led him out on a rope and tied him to a huge tree next to the fort. While wrapped together with this living thing, Taukolexis poured out his sorrow to the tree. He found relief in joining his spirit with that of the tree; it was his only consolation before death.

Taukolexis grew emaciated with malnutrition and torture; and with no support or hope of liberation, he died. If he could have held out a few hours longer, his story would have changed.

On July 14, 1696, just after Taukolexis died, a man named D'Iberville, with three armed ships and two battalions of French soldiers, anchored at Pemaquid. With the help of two hundred Tarratines in canoes led by the French officer Castin, he posed a massive threat to the fifty or so English fighters at the fort.

The attackers brought heavy guns and ammunition ashore, and batteries raised, projected many bombshells into the fort. Crabb quickly surrendered, and the opposition scrambled up the hill to the garrison. The Frenchmen strutted valiantly, but the Indians, upon finding dead Taukolexis in such a deplorable condition, raised their weapons in fearsome anger. Fortunately for the English, they had already abandoned the fort.

The Tarratines removed the fellow member of their race from his chains, and brought his body to Tappan Island. There they buried him in a fashion befitting an Indian brave, with knees drawn up and head facing east. Someone threw in a knife and hunting pouch so that he would be happy in the next Hunting Grounds.

Taukolexis may be happy there, but he visits his old "hunting grounds" every once in a while. After the tourists have trampled, the picnickers have lunched, and the fort keeper has locked up for the night, the spirit of the captured Indian appears. A white wisp of light has been seen coming out the restored fort's door, moving towards the big tree nearby, according to a retired engineer.

One gate tender, upon closing shop for the night, noticed a man coming towards him in haste. In the split second of realization, there was a sense of deep sadness about the person. He was also walking a foot above the ground. The gate tender did not stop to question why; he got to his car as quickly as possible and took off.

A young woman, taking a nightly stroll last summer, ended up at the fort towering above the sea. It was a windless night, the air felt calm. Suddenly a cold wind brushed her; it stopped. It happened again. She reached up to her head and her hair was standing straight on end. Bewildered, she left the scene totally freaked out.

Just before the fort is a sign that reads Makooshan Tribe #4—Everybody Welcome! The people who made that sign are not afraid of the ghostly visitor. They communicate with him, no qualms. As Willie Nelson would say, they've "been down that road before."

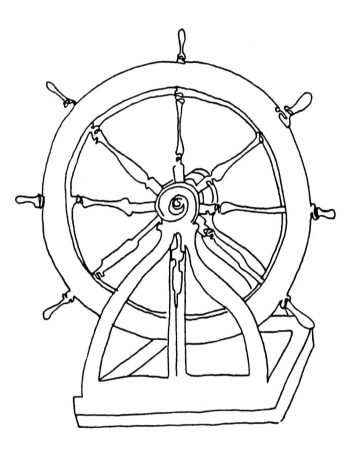

(74)

CHAPTER TWELVE

ROSES FOR A QUEEN

It has long been a mystery why, in certain old homesteads of the Boothbay region, one would find a Sevres vase or delicately painted snuff box or graceful-legged Louis Quinze chair amid the lusterware, the willow plates, and the sturdy captain's tables. Even more astounding is the discovery of fleshy, voluptuous females in paint, prancing around with bewigged men and chubby cupids. Surely such a picture hanging in a puritanical nineteenth-century home would have been cause for eternal damnation for the whole household.

There's an old saying that if you live in a place long enough, you will hear the end of every story. Such is the case with the late eighteenth-century French antiques. It revolves around one large but unpretentious white frame house with green shutters, in the town of Edgecomb. It was, in 1793, a house prepared for a woman of very high breeding and meticulous taste.

The episode must be prefaced by a portrayal of the man involved. Arthur Clark was a tough-minded, independent Yankee, one of the elite "first family" members of Boothbay. The town of Boothbay was so commercial with its ship chandleries, shipping offices, warehouses and taverns, that people like the Clarks chose for their homes quiet little places like Edgecomb.

Arthur was a versatile fellow, as most captains were, in those days. He not only commanded his vessels, he also owned them and the shipyard where they were built. Such a position of responsibility fostered the strict, practical side of his personality. Thus, the events that took place on his ship in the fall of 1793 came as quite a surprise to his crew.

Captain Clark was docked just outside of Paris at the time, with his ship *Sarah*. Any persons in the vicinity of this city of revolution had to be touched in some way by the social upheaval going on around them. Angry Parisian mobs, going hungry while their rulers glutted themselves with pleasure, thronged the streets and shouted their grievances. The fire of their nightly torches matched the fire in their eyes.

It was the fourth year of captivity for the reigning monarch, Marie Antoinette. Her husband Louis XVI had lost his head during the winter, and the memory of her recently deceased son still lingered. All attempts to procure aid from her Austrian family had failed. The French people were labeling her with treason, because it was believed that during the previous year's war she had passed on military secrets to the enemy. She could no longer take advantage of her luxurious palace at Versailles, but she was able to take comfort in what was left of her elaborate clothes, sculptured furniture, expensive wallpaper, and priceless wall hangings. Albeit a set of inanimate objects, it was all she had left.

This was the story told by the delicate and forlorn queen to the hardy sailor from Maine, who had somehow managed to meet her. Captain Clark was so taken by this damsel in distress that he quickly formulated a plot by which she could escape. Little by little, her belongings were stowed away on his ship by his loyal crew. Clark's sailors must have given him quite a ribbing about this romantic adventure, but they were smart enough to realize the stakes involved. For all practical purposes, Marie Antoinette was under house arrest, and anyone found tampering with the situation would have been in danger of his life.

Clark, being a man of the sea, was used to taking chances, but he was not used to sympathizing with royalty. During the American Revolution he had been a staunch patriot and a loud condemner of the British ruler's atrocities. One can imagine the shock when Mrs. Clark learned that her husband planned to rescue the French queen and give her refuge in his own home in Edgecomb. I'll bet she slammed a few pots and pans around the kitchen whenever she thought of the sentimental scheme. How would a lady used to fancy French cooking look upon fish chowder and johnnycakes? How would she feel at home in a plain two-story dwelling? How far would she look down her nose at a Maine sea captain's wife? Most of all, was it worth the terrible risk?

Mrs. Clark's concerns and all of Edgecomb's female society's preparations were for naught. Just as the captain's plan was living out its final stages, whereby the queen would go to the ship in disguise, violence broke out. Marie Antoinette was seized and beheaded on October 16. *Sarah* had to leave port immediately, with no time to unload her cargo of French treasures.

The captain stored them for a time in one room of his house, awaiting word from French authorities. When none came, he distributed them about the house, I suspect, in spite of his wife's protests. Then in a final tribute to the woman he loved in some way, he planted a trellis of roses facing the morning sun.

Herbie, the present gardener of the house, was the one so willing to relate information about the lovely roses and the story behind them. Most of the antiques have been sold or distributed as far as the Metropolitan Museum of Art, but evidence of his tale still remains. He first experienced it ten years ago, at one of the many auctions held at the home.

He had always heard stories of how Marie Antoinette was still looking for her lover, but he'd never seen anything. Then one hot and windless summer afternoon during that auction, on the side of the house where there was no activity, he was passing by the roses. He took great care of those roses. Anyway, he was walking by when he caught sight of a miniature whirlwind that traveled twice

(78)

around the foot of the trellis and then went right up it. He never saw anything like it in his life.

Herbie said that Morris, the gardener before him, had told him a story about his sleeve being tugged while working on the roses. When Morris looked up to see no one, he dropped his tools and went for a long walk.

Morris said that the French queen never got to see those roses while she was alive, but she certainly seems to know that they're hers now.

CHAPTER THIRTEEN

MUSICAL MYSTERY HOUSE

n the prim and proper, neatly windowed town of Wiscasset lies a Georgian manor that seems to fit in with all the other 1850s vintage homes. The brick sidewalk by the old Congregational Church leads the way to a double-doored immensity that signals a definite "welcome" to the passersby. Candlelight softens the entrance to the house, and one step inside tells you that this is no ordinary place.

Alfred Hitchcock would have gone wild. Instead of the grand mirrors and Victorian chairs that usually adorn a hallway of this sort, stands a ceiling-high display of antique musical mechanisms. They range from three-inch music boxes to Aeolian pneumatic organs. The preponderant taste seems to be German, as seen in the tall glassed symphonium supported by sturdy carved legs, and the Black Forest creatures with real animal horns.

The pleasant but ethereal cacophony of several instruments playing at once shifts one's mind away from the everyday world and into another dimension. The key to this dimension strolls into the hallway and lifts his head in a manner that suggests heavy back pain. Thick eyebrows shade dark eyes that dispel seriousness more quickly than expected. He does not resemble anything that exemplifies Down East Yankee.

His name is Josef Schmidt, and he is the keeper of this musical fantasy land. Josef does not have to collect and maintain these precious items; he does it because he loves to. An outsider's eye, however, would detect that there is so much passion involved in the project, that the loving force has driven him to make the whole thing a necessity. His collection began in Washington, D.C., but the house there became too small. He expanded his musical storehouse to a Maine resort town and Dallas, Texas. Then he bought the house in Wiscasset, and now this building is not big enough to hold the ever-increasing displays.

The operation of the music boxes is easily understood, but that of the mechanical organs and pianolas raises questions. He explains that he does not "play" the instruments; he interprets the heart and soul of the music by means of the foot pedals. As the player Steinway is pumping out notes written by Mozart and recorded by a professional pianist, Schmidt controls the pace and temperament of the piece. Closing his eyes in complete concentration, he becomes the captain who steers the ship or the artist who frames the lovely painting. Sometimes, when no one is around, "someone else" plays the instruments, he says with a wink.

Dismissing the remark in good humor, all those following Schmidt around to different rooms continue up the flying staircase. A set of broad tuckered drapes decorates a gold-and-black bedroom. A candlelight chandelier with diamond drop pendants illuminates a somber black bed that looks more like a throne. The heavy night stands sustain golden bowls that once held washing water for their historic owner, the Archduke of Austria. After five motley peasant figures dance atop their music boxes, the group listens to a short concert on the bedroom pianola, composer unknown. Schmidt makes the music sing throughout the house. He delights in this piece even more than the Mozart.

Part of the group leaves him still playing while others peek into various rooms, curious about the ivory knobs, the three-foot brass cylinders and the carved cases of the automata. The shapes range from huge clocklike structures to three birds in a gilded cage, warbling a foreign anthem. One woman finds a small cubbyhole of a room.

She steps into it gingerly as the floorboards creak underneath her feet. The place is fascinating because there is something about it unlike the other rooms. It feels private; it definitely "belongs" to someone. She walks over to the twin music boxes that serve as platforms for two German beer drinkers but chooses not to turn the keys. An inlaid bookcase is more interesting, with its dusty old books and little brown globe. She was perusing the weatherworn map of Europe on the wall when a rustling noise to the left caught her attention. The books on the shelf were falling on each other, one by one to the right, as though someone were riffling through the stacks. One of the books sort of flew out and dashed itself at her feet, making her sneeze with the dust. In that moment the music box keys turned in their sockets and the mechanisms started playing their different tunes.

The woman, too shocked to scream, made a low, frightened sound and quickly backed out the door. Upon shutting it, she realized that she had not observed the white sign that read No Public Admittance. In order to keep from being scolded, she did not relate this incident to the owner, but she started telling it to the rest of her party, as she ushered them out the main door. The music eerily continued through the closed door of the little room.

Right after she left, the owner stopped playing the pianola and came downstairs to check on the room in question. "Just as I thought," he said. "Someone's been in here, because I left this door open. Was it you?" He looked at the person nearest the door. By this time a small crowd had gathered. The accused answered negatively, but she told him what had happened to the woman who had just left. Josef nodded knowingly, and as he opened the door to pick up the book, a cold draft escaped, rippling through the onlookers.

"This is my grandfather's room," he lectured. "I've been keeping it for him. As a matter of fact, I've been keeping this whole collection for him." He gestured abstractly.

Hans Reutenberg, it turned out, was a musician

and composer in the late nineteenth century. Music was his whole life. His son carried on family tradition by becoming a music box restorer. Handel, Bach, and Beethoven discs were his favorite. In 1957 Reutenberg's grandson, Josef, after moving to America, cultivated an emotional link with the grandfather, and started collecting mechanisms on which Hans's music could be played. It was a Reutenberg composition that had been tinkling its way through the house at Josef's hands, from the Austrian bedroom—another German gift of probably the greatest spiritual enhancement of all, music.

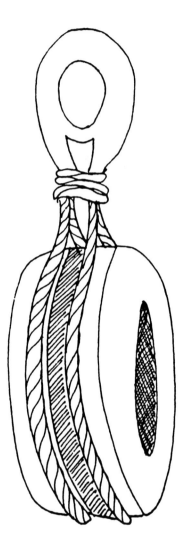

(86)

CHAPTER FOURTEEN

BATH BUILDER

So many ghosts were people with strong personalities and a great deal of energy. This energy breaks through the material world, even from the non-material plane of existence, even after many "years" of being on this plane. I say "years" because it is my opinion that "time" in this sphere is a totally different concept, most likely not the linear version that we Westerners are accustomed to.

These high-powered people made big impressions on their communities and on the communities to come. In the town of Bath, shipbuilding capital of the world, it would be difficult to encounter an outstanding person not connected with this industry. It would be like trying to find an Iowan not attached in some way to agriculture.

Even now, although the aromas of molasses, tar, resin, and pine are not intermingled with the basic smell of the sea, Bath products are among the best boats in the country. In place of the schooners and barks so handsomely docked in the past stand sleek gray destroyers, laden with the sophisticated radar necessary for present-day navigation in the Persian Gulf, for example. Many of the men working on these ships are descendants of those who built the first Bath vessels. They claim that the spirit of their forebears permeates the waterfront.

The best place to encounter this sort of thing, they say, is the Bath Maritime Museum, a preservation of the original buildings of the great shipyards. The men are busy with their work, but they take time to joke about the ghost stories that have been circulating for years.

Not one to be daunted by friendly ridicule, I traveled with my family over to the museum to see what I could find. The boat nearest the Caulking Shed was the one we picked to explore. The *Sherman Zwicker* was a small schooner constructed on the principles of nineteenth-century shipbuilding. Below deck every space was well-utilized, and it seemed cramped and dark—a great place for a ghost hideout. My husband made the remark that it would make you think twice about going to sea. I reminded him that this boat was quite a bit smaller than the original schooners, and besides, people back then were of a smaller stature. There are pictures on the walls of old houses that show plenty of space below deck: a niche for a berth, a partition containing a six- or seven-foot harmonium and another space for a private water closet. Of course, that would have been the captain's quarters.

We visited the Mold Loft, the Mill and Joiner Shop where there was part of an old shipwreck, the building for small craft which included a dugout canoe, and the Apprentice Shop where new boats are in the making. Most of the buildings were dark and creepy, but there was no sign of a ghost.

The city heat and humidity began to wear on our nerves, and we were on our way out when I said, "Wait a minute, let me check out this building." It was the Paint and Treenail (pronounced trunnel) Shop. The kids tagged along after me while my husband waited outside.

Nobody else was in the place. It seemed darker and older than the other buildings. Three anti-quated engines stood inside the door, then a pulley display, and a large wooden style operated by manpower, used for hauling or rigging. In the corner was a display of shipyard store items, and to the side, a ten-foot wharf scale.

The kids were in front of me and the scale behind. The solemnity of the place was broken by a large squeak and the sound of metal. We all turned toward the scale. Whereas before it had been a foot off the ground, it was now resting on the ground. Suddenly it popped up again.

As we turned toward the store items, a bowler hat sitting atop a metal safe camouflaged as a desk moved and landed on top of an antique cash register. The kids left immediately, but I had to get the name on the store display: Hefflin. Mr. Hefflin meant no harm. He was just saying "hello" (tipping his hat?). I moved to a book in the center of the shop to find out the story behind the elusive presence.

Lucas Hefflin came to Bath, then called Long Reach, in 1792 at the age of nineteen. After marrying Harriet Rowe, he produced five sons, all of whom helped their father sustain the family businesses. From a general merchandise store selling ladies' and children's shoes, Lucas graduated to the big-time merchant business and became an importer.

Spurred on by success, he took shares in several Kennebec-built vessels. By 1815 he reigned over his own shipyard, from which were launched four brigs, three barks, and seventeen ships. In 1825 Lucas expanded his waterfront holdings to include a third wharf and a store. Ten years later he purchased more property, and more in 1846 and 1854. In 1854 he also added another wharf and a brick store that became his oakum and paint shop.

Hefflin gained popularity as a man who gave employment to many men and kept the town going with his generosity. One day in 1857 the ship *Hefflin*, coming into port after an overseas journey, seemed to sense that this well-loved leader had passed away the night before. She breezed in silently, waving her flags at half mast for the man who had watched her progress from the laying of her keel to her complete construction and worthiness at sea.

Today, it seemed, Mr. Hefflin was sticking around to watch over the growth and development of the fifth generation of his family in the ship-building business. Was it one of the fellows who had talked to me at the shipyard down the street? As I pondered this, I felt a pressure like a footprint start at the back of my left ankle. I could feel it slowly work its way up my back till it got to my hair. It either pulled my hair or caused static electricity. Time for me to split.

As we drove by the boat workers on the way back, they asked if we'd had any luck finding ghosts. "One of you guys named Hefflin by any chance?" I asked. They pointed to a fellow about thirty feet away. I said, "Tell him to visit the Paint and Treenail Shop sometime," and we drove off.

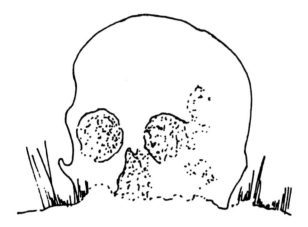

CHAPTER FIFTEEN

SALLY WEIR

There are no accidents. This theory does not rule out free will; it merely states that everything that happens comes from within us. Subsequently, it was no surprise to us when two women and I met at a meeting in Northport. They were being bothered by a ghost, and I was researching stories for this book. Thus began the chapter of the most twisted, entangled mass of information I had encountered so far.

Terry and Amanda, residents of Bucksport, are mother and daughter. Mandy is a fresh-faced girl with dark blond hair, her large ocean eyes framed by strong bones leading down to a healthy jaw. A full mouth expands into a smile that would not go unnoticed by any teenage lad I know.

She has been having horrible dreams about a faceless woman crying for help underwater. In the dreams Mandy, with her boyfriend in scuba gear behind her, reaches out to help the woman, but to no avail. She describes the woman as fiftyish with dirty blond hair and an old-fashioned dress with buttons open at the bosom. The recurrent nightmare persisted to such a degree that the girl asked her mother for help. "Mom, I have to find out who this woman is."

Terry, a bright little energetic hairdresser, took on the case. Together mother and daughter dug into historical records and asked a lot of questions around town. Through an old newspaper article that included a picture, they determined that Sally Weir was the woman. The description of her burial place was so confusing, however, that no one could tell them where to look for it. Her place of burial was not the only confusing issue. The manner of her death was as bizarre as it was bewildering. At our meeting they asked me to join the search. I agreed, and the following is what we learned.

Sally Weir, divorcee and hard-working woman of the late 1800s, found that her only means of support in the town of Bucksport was employment as a domestic. Mrs. Milo and the Bolder brothers were her chief employers. Sally, who bore a striking resemblance to Amanda, especially about the jaw, had talents above and beyond the role of chambermaid, and here the resemblance ends. Her mind encompassed the man's world of politics, legal matters, and illegal matters such as bootlegging and prostitution. She gave advice on all of these subjects, usually with a sense of humor and a thin cigar stuck in her mouth.

Sally was the life of the party September 17,

1898, the night of a poker game held at Mrs. Milo's house. After much drinking and guffawing by the four male players, she laughingly acknowledged herself as the "stakes" of the game. Then this fifty-two-year-old good-looker went about her business. She would soon be the death of the party.

Let's take a look at the partygoers. Terry found out that they included two lawyers, the Bolder brothers; Tom Treelee, a store owner; and Ed Finn, a town selectman. These men formed a card-playing club that met every Saturday. They also formed part of a group of men engaged in the bootlegging and possible prostitution trade of a local tavern.

Tom Bolder was the more vibrant of the brothers. You wouldn't want to go against him in a courtroom; his brilliant oratory would beat you every time. He was also a bit of a rogue, especially since he'd been widowed, and when he got drunk he could out-talk and out-punch any of the lot. George was older, and protective of his brother. It was his self-appointed task to cover up whenever Tom messed up. Ed Finn was a merchant and family man; Treelee was a good man, not very bright.

There are three versions to the next part of the story. One is that after the poker game, Sally left Mrs. Milo's house with sixty-five dollars that she had just been paid. She then purchased a two-cent cheroot at Bogg's Store and went across the street to the Bolders', where she did some light housework for them. Again she was paid. While on her way back through the brush to Mrs. Milo's (for she did not want to leave the old lady alone that night), either one of two things happened. She was accosted by an unknown attacker who killed her for the money, or she committed suicide.

The second version is that Sally was killed at Mrs. Milo's house, the night of the poker game, and dragged through the overgrowth to the spot where she was located eighteen days later.

Our version states that Sally had aroused the angry and/or sexual passions of Tom Bolder, winner of the poker game. She left Mrs. Milo's to replenish the supply of her favorite smokes, and Tom followed. They may have stopped at Tom's house for small talk or the pillow talk that was supposedly the prize at the end of the game. In any case, they left there and walked through the brush in continuance of whatever they had started in the house. Tom's anger got the better of him and he murdered Sally not for money, because he had plenty of that. He killed her because she knew enough about his underhanded dealings in town to have him arraigned, should she desire revenge. Maybe he got too rough with her sexually, and she threatened to spill the beans.

This version is the one we cling to, because of the undisputed state of her body. The authorities found the left ear (everything she heard) totally severed, as well as her mouth (whatever she could tell). No doubt as to a crime of passion. The bones in front of the left ear were gone, and a portion of her upper and lower jaws and cheekbone were not only broken, but broken off and missing.

Also, circulation of the first version enforces a robbery motive, while the second version puts at least four people under equal suspicion. We believe that these tales were concocted as part of a giant coverup to protect a prominent community citizen.

When Sally's body was lifted to be put on the morgue cart, her head fell off and had to be boxed separately. The skull, badly fractured and sharply nicked in four places, was used at the trial as evidence of murder. After the trial it was placed in the Ellsworth Courthouse safe, where it remained untouched by human hands. No one had opened that box since 1898. We were the first to investigate the small piece of mutilated head.

The clerk of the court told us who took the rap for the crime: simple-minded Tom Treelee. He was paid a tidy sum for his services. No one could tell us what became of Mr. Treelee. It is ironic that his surname is engraved on the cornerstone of the courthouse, this monument to the pursuit of justice.

When I turned over the skull to check out the back of it, Terry choked with fear. There on a seam going down the back was wedged a brown hair. Underneath it were about eleven short blond hairs, sticking straight out of the skull. Terry, having studied cosmetology, told us that hair needs living tissue to subsist. She could not believe that we were witnessing healthy human hair on a ninety-year-old skull. Maybe this was Sally's way of telling us that in some sense she was still "alive." The whole DA's office came down for a look.

This incident was an impetus for discovering the truth about the rest of her body. Was it buried alongside her Weir in-laws in the town cemetery?

There is a gravestone bearing her name, but we think not. Was it buried in a crypt by the lake? It seemed a likely location, since townspeople have always spoken of a female ghost wisping about Silver Lake on foggy evenings.

We all walked down to the lake and were immediately drawn to it. There was an old crypt lodged in a small incline, but we disregarded it because we were drawn to the lake itself. Terry said that when she was a kid, she was always afraid to skate on a certain part of the lake—not because of thin ice, but because that area creeped her. Amanda had come here twice before, in search of Sally.

My attention focused on an area of the lake right in front of us, about fifty yards out. Every time I looked at that spot, thunder rolled. It was not cloudy, nor did it ever storm the rest of the day. Mandy drew agitated breaths. We threw a stick in the water. It pointed directly to the spot.

Why would Sally be underwater? Convinced of our intuitions, we went back to the Historical Museum in town. On one of the old brown walls hung a map that described a cemetery where Silver Lake now stands. In 1930 the new Bucksport factory needed that tract of land for water supply. The plant hastily dug up whatever bodies it could, and placed them ashore in various crypts, before making its man-made reservoir. In the process, it must have overlooked Mrs. Weir.

Today she cries out to have her body reunited with her imprisoned skull. Only a judge's decision can release it. While driving past Silver Lake for the last time that day, we spied the most dominant gravestone in the cemetery on the hill overlooking the lake. It was inscribed with the name "Tom Bolder." Perhaps and rightly so, it is also his fate to be witness to the haunting figure of Sally Weir stalking Silver Lake.

CHAPTER SIXTEEN

WILLIE CUNNINGHAM'S CAT

t is scary enough for a human being to witness a forest fire racing down a mountain towards his home. Imagine a poor animal in this circumstance, its sharp instincts smelling nothing but smoke, fear, and confusion all about her. Such was the case of Willie Cunningham's cat in the 1947 fire that devastated Bar Harbor.

Bar Harbor, a summer resort of affluent rusticators since the 1890s, awoke the morning of October 21 to a column of smoke that had turned into a major conflagration. Having started in the area of the dump, it had jumped outside the fire line, its flames lapping the over-dry trees of the autumn drought. It snapped and crackled out of control to such an extent that the Parisian newspapers picked up the story.

By the twenty-first, five fire departments and two hundred soldiers from the Bangor army base were working to stop the disaster. A crew of native residents added its strength to the effort. When they saw some stray sparks land on a barn roof, burst it into flames and shoot embers into the parched woods beyond, they felt grim. In that instant the fire had begun to move uphill, away from the sea.

After lugging shovels, picks, and fire hoses to the scene, firefighters pumped water from a nearby lake. The heat kept moving them back. The soles of their feet burned and their hair and eyebrows were singed. Their toils didn't amount to much. It was just like spitting into a furnace.

These blackened men staggered back to the Bar Harbor firehouse for relief, but there were too few men for so much fire. Soon the blaze was moving south into Acadia Park, north toward Hull's Cove, and east directly towards town.

Millionaires' Row was next. The mansion of J.P. Morgan burned right down to its massive stone arched foundation. The summer cottages of people in the same class as the Rockefellers, Kents, Vanderbilts, and Pulitzers were totally destroyed. One "cottage" lost all eighty rooms, including doors with gold doorknobs, and twenty-six living rooms with marble fireplaces.

Fortunately, most of these estates were vacant after summer, so loss of life was not a consideration. Lost, however, was the extensive grandeur and high life of a whirlwind social clique that thrived on gourmet dinner parties, sixty-foot yachts, and dancing balls with famous orchestras. Out of sixty-seven wealthy property owners, only a handful returned to Bar Harbor to restore their homes.

It is not the woes of the super rich community, however, upon which this story focuses. As the fire moved nearer town, it threatened to become a death trap for twenty-five hundred year-round villagers. The thick yellow smoke formed a tidal wave of heat that blistered the paint off cars trying to escape. Men, women, and children fled screaming down the streets.

In the area of the ball field, the most valiant town members, along with the National Guard, were going around in trucks, picking up the elderly, the disabled, and anyone who could not evacuate themselves. The plan was to round up everyone in the field and walk them to the municipal wharf, six blocks away. There rescue boats, Coast Guard, and fishing boats would transport them to safety. The exodus was compared to Dunkirk.

To the right of the ball field was a modest one-story house with a comfy front porch and a wooden swing. Old Willie Cunningham was just stumbling out the front door with his black cat "Seawater," when he heard something that sounded like a freight train roaring in the wind. The smoke caught his breath and doubled him over in a coughing fit, but he held on to his cat all the while.

Willie was good with animals. He knew what made them tick—what they liked to eat, how they reacted to things, what they shied away from. This natural knowledge helped him a great deal out on the fishing waters by Gott's Island. He was the best Bar Harbor fisherman of his day. Lately he hadn't done much, being laid up with rheumatism, but he could tell colorful stories about the adventures he and Seawater had experienced out to sea. There was the time she had a gruesome fight with a giant crab that had escaped from a lobster trap Willie had just hauled. There was the time Seawater led them home through the fog with her head pointing the way.

His hearing hadn't been so good, so the whole scene taking place in front of his doorstep took him aback some. An olive green truck swerved around the corner and screeched to a halt. Two husky men hustled Willie and his cat to the back of the truck and lifted them on. They hadn't gone but a block when the cat jumped out of Willie's arms and panicked towards the house. Before anyone could stop him, Willie jumped out, too. That was the last anyone saw of the man and his animal.

The fire continued on and torched the famous cancer research center, the Jackson Laboratory, wiping out one year of Pulitzer prizewinning work. That day it covered over five miles in three hours, devouring thirteen thousand acres—nine thousand more than it had traveled in the past two days. As it started to pour down on the town, the wind made a freak shift and turned it in another direction.

A week passed before the blaze was dominated. It still glowed between cracks in the rocks until November 14, when the fire was officially declared "out," and people were allowed to return. Many Bar Harbor residents came back to burnt rubble where their homes had once stood.

Willie's neighbors were checking what was

left of his foundation when they discovered a pile of human bones sitting in the corner. One of the men looked up and spotted a black cat circling the ruins. He called it and it stopped; he went to chase it and it vanished into nothingness.

For a while after that, people talked about seeing "Willie's cat" looking around for her beloved master. Sometimes it kept children awake with its mournful meowing on moonlit nights. Other times it just prowled the spot where Willie had reached out for the last time to try to help his little pet.

(106)

CHAPTER SEVENTEEN

JESUIT SPRING

 cadia National Park's Flying Mountain serves as a headstone for eight Jesuit missionaries murdered in October 1613. It stands tall above the spot where the victims, along with a small colony of settlers and lay brothers, were assaulted by a man on a fishing expedition. This man, in a brutal surprise attack, totally destroyed the Jesuit Mission, the first white settlement on Mt. Desert Island. The unmarked graves lie along the western shore of Somes Sound, a place not only haunted by the shades of the holy men, but also disturbed by the unceasing patter of a freshwater spring.

Jesuit Spring is what the natives call it. Guarded by forest pines and sturdy boulders, it spills into the blue-green water that laps on the sand of a small beach. You won't find many islanders walking this beach. They don't like to tread on sacred ground. Some even claim that spring changes to a different color every once in a while—an unmistakable blood red.

The scene of the slaughter takes us back to the court of a French noblewoman, the Marquise de Boucherville, in March of 1613. This daughter of Catholicism counseled two Jesuits, Fathers DuPain and Rousseaux, to get on the next ship to Port Royal, Nova Scotia, and tend to the spiritual needs of the French colony there. Why? Religious fervor is one answer. Also, because the French church and state were closely aligned, the marquise's action strengthened France's foothold in the New World. Religious principles aside, the possibility remains that a dashing sailor with a heartbreaking smile who had been frequenting the French court took off for Nova Scotia, and she wanted to keep tabs on him.

Whatever the case, the two priests were not a big hit upon arrival at Port Royal. The rough and ready Nova Scotians told them to go back to Paris, where there was enough unholiness to attend to. The Jesuits wrote back to their sponsor to tell her the story. Not wishing her well-financed plan to go completely awry, she recommended that they gather their lay brothers, laborers, and animals and set their sights for Penobscot Bay. According to her, hoards of Indians were sitting there just waiting to receive the Catholic faith, and consequently, French politics. With this in mind, the missionary band of hopeful settlers said goodbye to Nova Scotia and sailed merrily upwind.

Nature, that devious force so often overlooked by those not in tune with the earth, took a hand.

The Maine fog, totally foreign to the Jesuit ship, enveloped the vessel and caused it to mistakenly land on Mt. Desert Island. The travelers chalked it up as part of God's plan, and promptly set about establishing a mission. Little did they realize that in three short months the whole place would be ashes.

The perpetrator of the disaster was just a guy doing his job, a policeman on duty. Arlan Seawall didn't ask for the job, but the London merchants were so dazzled by his deeds of exploration in the New World, that they appointed him Admiral of Virginia. The letter from the Virginia Company stated that Captain Seawall was to patrol the coast and try to prevent any settlements by the French.

England and France were not at war in 1613, so bloodshed was not expected. Mediation and peace talks were the tools of the day. Either Seawall's instructions were misunderstood, or the captain overreacted to a non-threatening situation.

One day, fishing down the coast, he spotted the little unprotected mission built on a flat, grassy peninsula. He yelled to his crew, who left their nets and wasted no time bombarding the building to pieces. The English artillery and expertise far outweighed that of the religious scholars, who tried unsuccessfully to shoot back with a lone cannon. The Jesuit "cannoneer" was so inept that the weapon backfired and helped destroy part of the mission.

By the time the smoke had cleared, eight men lay dead, and the remaining hardy souls were taken aboard as slaves to be sold. Those not fit to sell would be set free in small boats in the middle of the ocean, where they would soon perish.

Seawall's men prowled the shore and scoured the ruins. When they came upon the spring, they refreshed their thirsty throats and decided that it was a place good enough for a cemetery. They wanted to get going, but they were God-fearing enough to supply Christian burial to the priests. Besides, these Puritan Englishmen regarded Papists with such absolute horror that they considered them nigh instruments of the Devil.

Devil's advocates or not, a place spirited by men of the cloth is a formidable place to be. The children of the area will tell you that they have been warned as such. Many tales have they heard about night fishermen seeing white shapes flitting about Jesuit Spring. One kid said that last year his father was out rowing when he saw a man in brown holding a cross to his chest. He took in his oars and grabbed his glasses to get a better look, but the "man" was nowhere to be seen.

Boats do not dock on the shore by Jesuit Spring, especially since the summer of 1975. It was then the Colby family loaded their sixteen-foot skiff with swimsuits, towels, and a picnic lunch. The water was without a ripple as they cruised along the shore. They spotted the pretty little beach with a freshwater stream pouring onto it and decided to land. Mr. Colby tightly wedged the anchor between two rocks. The tide was not quite in so they put the picnic stuff under a tree and looked up to Flying Mountain. A nice day for a hike, not too warm and no breeze.

The family climbed the mountain in about twenty minutes. When they came back down, there was no boat, no anchor, no snipped line, and no picnic basket—just the still clear water. Not a sound, not a movement. None of the nearby households had witnessed anyone else in the area although they had noticed the Colbys and all their doings.

The incident might have gone unnoticed or been passed off as robbery if two more boats hadn't met the same fate within a year. Besides, stealing is rare in coastal Maine, and when it does occur, everyone knows who did it and why.

The people of Mt. Desert know "who" took the boats, and they're not interested in talking about the why.

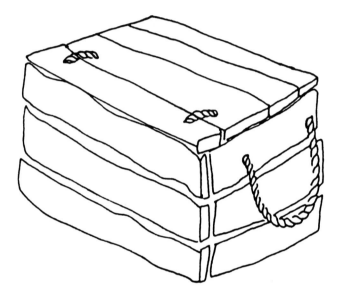

(112)

CHAPTER EIGHTEEN

JEWELL'S ISLAND

T he subterranean caves of Jewell's Island have not served savory purposes. Not only have they been conductors of smuggled goods, but they have also housed the secrets surrounding a lurid tale of buried treasure and cold-blooded murder.

Now a wild, uninhabited island, the place was once a quiet shelter for those who wished to live without constant fear of Indian attack. One has to think past the overhanging trees and jagged rocks to a time when people farmed the inland slopes and drew clear water from island springs. The eighteenth century had just begun.

Captain Elijah Jones was one of the first settlers to set the tone for this peaceful hideaway. When he wasn't shipping goods, he was tending his vegetable garden and two cows. He did not have a family, but like most islanders, he did not mind fending for himself.

If he had done more farming and less shipping, he might not have fallen prey to the greediness of the world outside Jewell's Island. While traveling to places like the West Indies, Spain, or Jamaica, Jones saw millions of dollars worth of luxury goods exchange hands, but he, the humble farmer, was on the outside looking in. Oh, how he'd love to be comfortably rich and be able to go anywhere he wanted anytime he pleased. There was even the chance that a wealthier lifestyle might attract a good woman who could breed him some descendants.

Jones shifted from shipping to smuggling. It was the only way he could break into the big time. Instead of patching up his barn, he threw his energies into rigging his house with secret compartments and passageways. Underground tunnels led to inconspicuous coves where crates of illegal goods passed hands. Barrels of Jamaican rum were stowed away in the night by men of foul language and filthy breath.

Outwardly, the captain posed a respectable image, and the islanders knew none the worse. They wondered why he neglected his farm, but they figured that business at sea was keeping him busy. Also occupying his mind at the time was the story of buried treasure that had begun circulating while he was away on one of his trips. It seems that a man from a foreign land had been poking about the island, pick and shovel in hand. He had not stated his purpose.

The captain's imagination tingled at the thought of a chest laden with coins and jewels, right there under his nose. He did some digging on his own but came up empty-handed. Years passed, Elijah remained satisfied with his illegal trade and had forgotten all about the visitor with pick and shovel—until one day coming into port he found a man waiting for him on the shore.

The man hailed from St. John's, Canada, and he had recently been given a treasure map by a dying black man who had serviced the captain of a pirate ship. This time the stranger, Mr. George Vigny, had come prepared, but he still needed a mariner's compass. Elijah Jones was the only islander who owned one. When he realized that between him and the stranger they had a good chance of locating the treasure, he lustily invited Vigny to visit his farmhouse. There they spent hours planning, conversing, and drinking some of Jones's best liquor. In the dark of the night they stole away, unnoticed by anyone.

The next day found Captain Jones puttering about his garden and milking his cows. Soon afterwards he went to sea and came back with a sizable sum of money, which started him on the road to being the richest inhabitant of the island. No one ever saw the stranger again, but it was presumed that he had sailed back home after his meeting with Jones.

Elijah died the most prominent citizen of Jewell's Island and was buried in grand style. By this time everyone had put the Canadian stranger out of their minds. Two months after Jones's funeral, things changed.

A farmer was plowing his acres down by the southeastern shore of the island, when he came across a skeleton on the edge of the woods. It was wedged between two rocks. The years of ice and snow and weather had disintegrated all identifiable clothing, but a silver ring lying with the bones carried a clue. The ring bore the initials "G.V." From all appearances, the Canadian had never made it home because a treasure had been found—and he had been murdered upon discovery of it! No wonder Jones had become rich so quickly; his wealth had not been acquired at sea, it had been acquired from the sands of Jewell's Island.

Vigny's murder began to make sense. That was the reason people had been witnessing weird visions in that area, the ghastly shape of a man with blazing green eyes and blood running out of his mouth and chest. Islanders thought perhaps they were seeing the spirit summoned to guard the buried treasure. They had poured fresh lamb's blood over the spot in an effort to quell the devilish haunt. Now they were beginning to suspect it was the spirit of the Canadian stranger.

The skeleton find also gave rise to an explanation for the paranormal activities around Elijah Jones's old place. A voice screaming out in the darkness, and the sight of chairs furiously moving about the kitchen had been experienced. One night a chair actually blew about the room and then burst through a window.

No one fixed the hole, and the broken window made noises from the house more audible. Neighbors were startled one night by a loud popping noise. Not knowing what to expect, they ventured near enough to see a liquid rushing over the wooden floor. The smell was very strong, very ripe. That was the end of their nocturnal investigation. The morning light induced sparks of courage, so they actually opened the front door and walked over to the soaked floor. Rum was the liquid. It had flowed out of a barrel hidden away in the wall. More barrels were found, and more secret places, whereupon they came to a series of tunnels that led to the shore. Thus was the true nature of Jones's character revealed and talked about for many years to come.

As for George Vigny, he is still angry about his untimely death and continues to make his presence known to those who dare trespass on Jewell's Island.

CHAPTER NINETEEN

THE CURSED FARM

Freeport's southeast wind blows the sunset sands of a large barren area extending the arm of Thomas Grayson's curse just a little bit farther. The time is the present. What was once a thriving farm has turned into a Sahara-like desert in the space of about one hundred years. There is no other place like it in the world, primarily because of its young age and also because it still sustains life. Seventy-foot birches and even an apple tree grow out of the sand, although they are so buried that they appear to be small bushes at ground level.

The curse was kind to the few remaining trees, but it totally wiped out any chance of survival by the last farmer who owned the land. The first farmer was Thomas Grayson. He was of muscular stock from his mother's side of the family, and he had inherited the long body and intelligent eyes of his father's side. Like most men of his era, it took

(119)

him till he was forty years old to have accumulated enough assets to be able to provide for a wife and family. In 1797 he bought a three-hundred-acre farm and married Elizabeth Donaldson.

Elizabeth died in 1815, leaving behind three teenage sons to help their father till the land. This they did with great energy, harvesting crops of potatoes, green vegetables, and hay. They cultivated the blossoming apple orchard and tended their herds of sheep and cattle. Blueberries and strawberries abounded. In the winter they cut down their choicest trees and sold the lumber to the railroad for a good price.

A year later the oldest boy went off to sea, and the middle one was about to follow on his heels. There was quite a discussion about that, but Tom, being a loving father, would not stand in the boy's way. Besides, Tom was becoming good friends with a widow lady named Hattie, who had a strapping teenage boy and a good head for business. Soon after the second son left home, Tom married Hattie.

Tom, his youngest son David, Hattie, and her son Jonas fostered a new family unit. By 1836 they were among the most financially stable of anyone in the community. That was the year Tom died, but before he died, he made Hattie promise to give the farm over to David. There was no legal record of this, because Tom distrusted lawyers, but he did trust Hattie to honor his wishes. She didn't. She gave the place to Jonas, and David moved away.

The farm went well for mother and son for

about fourteen years. Then one day Hattie noticed a saucer-sized spot of white sand by the barn. She thought it odd at the time but not important enough to bother her son about. Two weeks later that little spot had turned into a small mound, noticed this time by Jonas. The prevailing winds from the east had swirled the sand to form a peak, but what in the Devil's name had pushed it up and out of the brown soil?

The Devil's name entered Jonas's mind more than once as he fought to ground the sand with cut-up brush. In a few months, the mound had become a dune, and mother and son were filled with trepidation. Visitors remarked about the sand mass; they had never seen the like, amidst so many acres of fertile ground. Tongues wagged all over the place, some of them making mention of Tom's dying wish to have David own the property. Maybe if David had been allowed to work the land, this would not have happened.

The spirit of Thomas Grayson seemed to be more evident as time wore on. Jonas stayed awake nights listening to the wind, witnessing out his window the handiwork of an invisible force that kept pushing the sand out of the ground. Its sparkle glinted in the moonlight, as it spilled over the fruitful fields and vegetable gardens that had taken so much work to keep alive. Mornings found him too tired or too despairing to go and fight the sand. He had to spend more time building blockades than tending to the livestock.

The sand did not relent. After killing the farm flora, it played a waiting game with the healthy timbers that bordered the fields. It crept over the tree roots and settled in layers until the trees bent over and died. The wind made an eerie sound, whistling through all the dead trees.

By 1860 Jonas had sold almost all the land that remained normal, which was about half the property. No one wanted the desert land. His mother had died the previous year, and his enthusiasm for life was waning.

One morning in 1875, the old man looked out his door to find his plow totally buried. He tried to move the wagon, but it wouldn't budge. It too was a victim of the sand. Jonas went back to the house to pack his belongings, then turned his back forever on the land that had held such great potential.

The "farm" lay dormant for about fifty years. The desert grew to include eight hundred acres of valleys and dunes. Tall trees were underground, as well as half the barn, and the springhouse that used to supply cool storage for food. One twilight evening a couple from Massachusetts, prospective buyers, were inspecting the grounds. They were wading through the sand around the springhouse when they noticed a stone structure nearby, half buried. They uncovered the whole piece, then recoiled in terror. The structure was a sculptured head with huge pointed ears and a wide mouth. The facial expression was sinister, as if to say, "Hah hah hah, the joke is on you." As if that weren't enough of a bad omen, as they were leaving they heard what sounded like male laughter echoing across the dunes. The couple did not return.

When people visit the desert, they note the

shortened trees, the old barn, and the picture of the diabolical head that is now totally buried. The caretakers are constantly sweeping new sand out of the barn in hopes of keeping at least one relic uncovered. When asked what will be next, they shrug and say, "wherever the wind decides to blow."

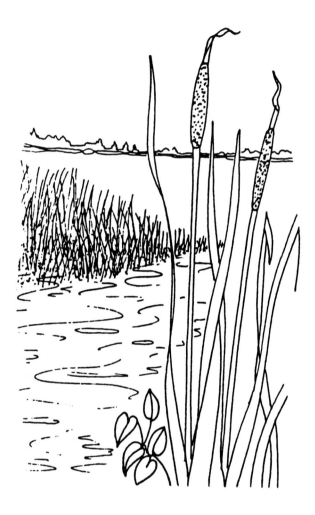

(124)

CHAPTER TWENTY

MASSACRE POND

I t is not surprising that a very disturbed ghost haunts Massacre Pond in Scarborough, formerly Black Point. Most of the west'ard (what Maine people call the coast from Kittery to about Portland) was at one time a veritable blood bath, the result of innumerable Indian/English battles. The account of one massacre pretty much sounds like that of another, except for the one in question that occurred on October 6, 1703. Massacre Pond is special because it was the culminating point in a series of tragic events that befell a certain man. This final incident in the life of Richard Stonewell gave the term "irony" new meaning.

His suffering began at age twenty-two after he had built his first family home, a three-room bungalow on Black Point River. He happened to be away on business one afternoon when a group of Indians attacked the cottage. They scalped his wife, then held his infant son by the feet and beat his head against the living room timbers until he died.

Stonewell never recovered from the shock. Not only were the deaths themselves devastating, but the manner in which they occurred was overwhelming. The Indians inhabiting the state of Maine (which was then part of Massachusetts) in 1667 had not yet reached their breaking point with the English settlers. Out-and-out war was not distinguishable until 1675. Besides, the French paid much higher bounties for women and children captives; adult male scalps were the grand prizes.

The English were also in the scalp business, and they paid well too, but Dick Stonewell did not care about money when he abandoned farming and joined the military service. His heart was full of vengeance, and he vowed to kill every Indian he could get his hands on. One of his favorite means of attack was to crash Indian meetings with white settlers, peaceful or not. He'd burst through the door and shoot indiscriminately until he ran out of ammunition. The Indians came to know him as "Crazy Eye."

And many came to know him, Maine through Canada. Now that Dick did not have a family, he was free to travel, and he volunteered for commissions that took him far from Scarborough. In an expedition to St. John's, his Indian fighting was described as "passionate."

The practice of taking chances when other men didn't dare caused him injuries. From 1690 to 1696 Dick sustained several wounds in his right arm and one arrow through the thigh. By 1697 he was so disabled that he came back home and petitioned the General Court for monetary assistance. It was granted.

Stonewell turned from an active combatant to one who tended the cows that belonged to the Black Point Garrison. He and nineteen other men were tending the cows out by the pond one October morning when, unbeknownst to them, a band of two hundred Abenakis from Canada were crouching in the bushes, lying in wait. They had come in the name of Christ, who, they had been told by the French, had been crucified by the English. They had also come in the name of the French, their neighbors and comrades in the fur trade. It seems that the French hunters and trappers had much more in common with the Indians than the English farmers and shipbuilders. Thus, they were able to infiltrate Indian tribes and establish themselves as brothers.

The Abenakis had been waiting, still as the trees, since the night before, October 5. They had done without fire and elaborate meals and had crept so stealthily as to keep the dogs unaware of their presence. The Indians sprung from the brush in bands of three or four, and their tomahawks fatally cut the flesh of all the garrison men except one. Richard Stonewell, yellow-haired "Crazy Eye," was among the dead.

The tale of Dick Stonewell has been kept alive through appearance of his spirit roaming the pond's edge. A description of one of these appearances came from an unexpected source, a Scarborough librarian. She was writing a newspaper article about Mr. Stonewell and in the process of digging up all sorts of information on him. The character's deeds were so colorful to her that she visited his burial place out of curiosity. This venture brought her straight to Massacre Pond, because the Black Point Garrison did not take the time to transport the massacre victims to their home burial plots. The threat of a repeated ambush was too great for that.

Lindsay, the librarian, did not get off work in time to visit the place during the day. It was way after supper when she went down to the parking lot where a footbridge spanned the pond and eventually led to the public beach. In the middle of her trek across the bridge, a swift movement caught her eye. It was just a play of shadows, she thought. It moved again, but this time she braved a little closer. She parted the tall cattails to see lying on the ground an old-fashioned knife-like weapon. It was surrounded by a five-foot circle of freshly cut reeds. Fearing some sort of strange person lurking about, she ran back to the car and drove off.

Dick Stonewell continued to fascinate her, however, and one week later Lindsay made the trip again, this time with a flashlight. She never did turn it on. There in the light of a full moon, on the edge of the pond, stood a figure with terrified, bulging eyes, bloody sockets where arms once were, and an arrow sticking through his thigh. It was the pierced thigh that gave him away. Lindsay had no doubt that she was witnessing what must have been the last pose of Richard Stonewell. The thigh with the arrow was probably just a symbol of recognition. Ghosts who want their identity known will do such things.

I asked about the weapon she had seen on her first visit, but she said "that was it" for her. She wasn't going to go traipsing around that area again, looking for anything. She told me to talk to Dave Simmons, a lifeguard at the beach.

Mr. Simmons was on duty at the time, and very slow to speak, but he admitted seeing something strange back by the pond. He wouldn't tell me any more. He didn't have to. I could see by the expression on his face that the spirit of Richard Stonewell had reached out to him.

I wondered if the lifeguard had understood the ghost's plea for help in comprehending the violence that had so plagued his earthly existence.

(130)

CHAPTER TWENTY-ONE

MEADOWLARK PLACE

here is something about a 1760 sign moving in the breeze, a half-buried plow, and a horse's tethering ring embedded in moss-covered rock that strongly signals a ghostly presence. These things so drew my attention that I had to stop the car and have a look around. They were the tip of the iceberg. Down the lane that led past this rural setting lay a broad marsh of kelly green reeds at the base of a small white cemetery. The stones were leaning at difficult angles, probably out of proximity to such moist ground. Immediately magnetized, I plowed through some of the marsh before I realized that the cemetery was inaccessible. Now I had to find the meaning behind this mysterious attraction, and I knew that at least one of those stones held the key.

The house that went with the farm stood watch over the grounds that I had just explored, but it looked friendly. The woman inside, Barbara Pearson, recited the story that I was seeking.

(131)

Many years ago Ms. Pearson's ancestors prospered on the land that still supports the original house and barn built in 1760 by Thomas Jenkins. The Jenkins family fared well from the land that grew all their food, raised their sheep and cattle, and nourished their horses. They also made a substantial living from the sea that was barely visible at the end of the spacious property. Thomas Jenkins was the ablest and luckiest sea captain of Old Kennebunkport. He never lost a ship during his whole career. What he did lose was something more precious than a ship: his second youngest son.

Twelve-year-old Tim Jenkins had a quiet way of enjoying life. He'd find a walking stick and go exploring the woods behind his house, while his brothers wrestled in the dirt. He loved to collect things like rocks and some insects, although he never killed any toward that end. His biggest collection comprised items from foreign lands brought back from overseas by his father. Tim had an ivory-handled spoon from Africa, a delicately tooled leather pouch from Spain, and a wooden box valentine decorated entirely with tropical sea shells. (Barbara showed me the only remaining piece of that collection, the African spoon.)

Ms. Pearson's facts were so detailed because of two diaries, one left by the boy, the other by his mother. Tim's brown-inked words were at times illegible, but the handwriting showed strong sensitivity. A great deal of this sensitivity seemed to be directed toward a girl his age, Rebecca Easton.

Ms. Pearson continued: Rebecca was the

daughter of the man who lived next door to Jenkins. She was a pretty little thing who had exactly the same interests as Timothy. Growing up in a family full of brothers had made her somewhat of a tomboy, and she readily made friends with Tim. The only strange aspect of their friendship was that their families were not speaking to one another. A short while after Tom Jenkins had settled here, Mr. Easton had come along and laid claim to some land that supposedly belonged to Jenkins. It was the beginning of a feud that would not die, despite a much later intermarriage between the families.

Tim and Rebecca, therefore, had to have a secret friendship. Their favorite meeting spot was the big rock next to the stone wall that separated the families' properties. Tim would tie up his horse at the rock and wait for Becky to cross over the wall, onto the Jenkins side. There the two friends could sit unnoticed for quite a long time, or at least until the horse got antsy. They couldn't wait to tell each other the latest gripe of their respective households, and then laugh about how silly the whole thing was.

One day as Tim was plowing the small field down towards the water, he heard Becky's call, somewhat similar to a crow's. That was their signal for meeting. It must have seemed urgent to Tim, because he left the plow right where it was. Instead of crossing the wall at the usual place, the Eastons' sheep pasture, he started wading through the marsh, which of course was unbound. The marsh unexpectedly got too deep for him, and not knowing how to swim, he drowned.

His was the first marker to be erected on the Jenkins' cemeterial plot. The family was beside itself. In order to preserve Tim's memory even further, they left his plow stuck in the ground exactly as he left it, where it remains today.

So does Tim's spirit. More than once, Barbara's son Evan, who helps take care of the property, has felt the young ghost about. Once when Evan was pitching hay in the barn, the sun got so warm that he shifted his position about fifteen feet. There he continued his work until he got thirsty enough to put down the pitchfork and go outside to get a drink. Within a minute's time he returned but found the pitchfork standing upright, directly in the sunlight.

Another time Evan had finished grooming one of the horses and went down to the west end of the barn to tend to the second horse. He heard nothing out of the ordinary, and certainly no disturbance from the first horse. When he looked over, however, he found the first horse all bridled and ready to ride bareback—just the sort of thing a young boy would do.

In the many years they've lived on the place, Barbara has witnessed one odd thing. She has seen the tethering ring in the big rock flop back and forth all by itself. The oddest thing, though, was the time . . . Barbara asked Evan to tell the story.

Evan poured himself a strong one and seemed hesitant to talk. Maybe he thought that I wouldn't believe him. I tried my best to convince him that anything was possible as far as I was concerned, and finally he spoke.

The afternoon was in its last moments one June day, when Evan was mowing the small field down towards the water. He came upon Tim's plow and stood staring at it a few moments as he was sometimes wont to do. All of a sudden before his very eyes the plow began to shake, then shook some more until it reached a violent peak. Evan left the mower and ran up to the house. By the time he and his mother returned to the spot, it had started to rain in great pelting drops, like huge tears. It rained for two days like that. Nobody has seen anything like it before or since—except for the day of Tim Jenkins' funeral.

CHAPTER TWENTY-TWO

CRYSTAL MAGIC

t my sister's soiree last year, a pleasant woman with an infectious laugh sat down to tell me my fortune. Let me rephrase that. Samantha came over to me and sat down; we shared the same sense of humor, and before I knew it, she was fondling my wedding ring. It was a bus-man's holiday for her, because her livelihood was being a psychic. The diamond told her several things: 1) I would take on a large project similar to a teaching experience, that would bring me fame; 2) I should get a crystal; 3) I should go to some place in Maine (she couldn't pronounce the name). I told her the name that had popped into my mind, "Ogunquit." My voice was questioning, because I had never been to Ogunquit, and the place held no significance for me. "Ogunquit, yes, that's it," she replied, and she got up to leave. That was fun, I thought, gee fame and fortune, but it was just a party game and nothing more.

Samantha's words meant nothing until this summer when I started writing this book. Number one, I had begun a big project and whether or not it would be a teaching experience remained to be seen. It had certainly taught me a few things. Number two, I'd been nosing around for a crystal that might help heal my back. Number three, the choice of ghostly locations was up to me, and Ogunquit sounded like a good one.

My mother accompanied me to the west'ard, and we settled in at our night's lodging, an 1814 guesthouse. I knew that before we left the next day something would come up, but I didn't know how or where. It would happen in the house, that was for sure. The low-timbered ceilings and nineteenth-century artifacts exuded that feeling. Our hostess, without saying a word, felt the same thing.

Mom and I went downtown to dinner, which took much more time than expected because of the summer crowds on the roads and in the restaurant. When I asked the parking valet where to buy a crystal, he suggested I talk to Susie, the bar waitress. Susie directed us to a tiny shop down the road, but she cautioned me not to buy just any old crystal. "Make sure it's one that you're attracted to."

Not knowing exactly what that meant, we traveled down the over-populated road to the shop, where there was a line of people outside who had just been told that the place was closed. Mom and I looked in the window, tapped on it, and the manager let us in, to the surprise and dismay of all those in line. The man was cordial to us, but he did not let anyone else in. Every time I think about that, it amazes me.

Following intuition, I started picking up various quartz crystals and held each in my hand for a few moments. There were symmetrically shaped crystals and many with formations pleasing to the eye. I held a nondescript mass of crystal adorned with a small vein of fool's gold, and shortly afterwards a warmth shot through my hand, all the way up my arm. That was definitely the one in tune with my body chemistry.

That night, after getting ready for bed, I lay down and started rubbing the stone, passing it from palm to palm, just fooling around. I fell asleep with it in my hand. For the first part of what happened next, I cannot say whether I was awake or asleep or halfway in between.

All I know is that sometime during the night the figure of a man appeared before me. There were two shades of light that flitted in front of the bedroom fireplace, and then one shade disappeared, while the other materialized into the man. He wore a brown tweed suit with a waistcoat that held a gold pocket watch. His hair was brown and wavy and somewhat slick, while his mustache sheltered a kind mouth. He was a handsome man, in his thirties. He had a good-looking face and a gentle, soothing voice. The voice was making indistinguishable sounds, and it might have been the voice that awakened me.

Totally startled and very much awake now, because I remember being too scared to look at him directly, I reached over to wake up my mother in the adjacent bed. The man reached over and said, "Oh, please, don't do that." Whereas before, his voice had sounded as though it were coming directly from his mouth, now it seemed as though it were right inside my ear. Maybe he realized that I couldn't understand him at first, so he threw his voice over to my ear. It was loud, but very understanding.

My hand withdrew and I looked up at him in unabashed panic. He waved his hands and before departing said something like, "Never mind. Some other time." There was so much psychic energy in the room at this point that it burst forth and caused a huge thud. It was my mother. She had been thrown out of bed.

This kind of apparition aftermath had happened before. Many years ago right after a ghost had appeared to me, the kitchen stove had exploded and singed my grandmother's hair and eyelashes.

Making sure that the crystal was out of my hands and on the floor, I tried to rest, but sleep did not come easily after all the excitement. The next morning I was tired and disappointed that I had been too scared for the ghost to remain—but there was an added mystery. Who was the shade that did not materialize?

A trip to the local historical society pretty much narrowed down my ghost's identity to John Bakersfield, son of the original owner, and occupant of the house in the mid-1800s. There were no photographs, because not many pictures were taken in those days. People considered photography something akin to black magic.

Now for the mystery ghost. A-hah! It could very well have been the occupant who put two bullet wounds through his head. He would have been an agitated spirit, as suicides are known to be. Right then and there I counted my blessings. And another thing—I made sure always to know the whereabouts of my ghost "telephone," that powerful transmitter, the quartz crystal.

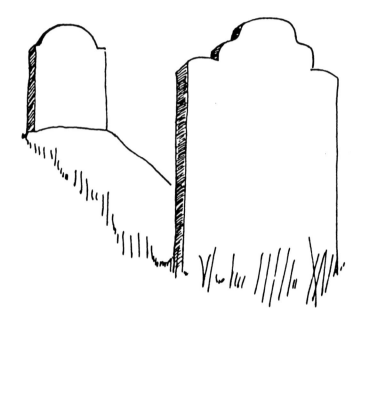

CHAPTER TWENTY-THREE

WITCH'S GRAVE

he woman was hard to find. She eluded me for at least an hour, while I perused Old York Cemetery and pored over volumes in the York library. I was chided for my search, by librarians and villagers alike. "Well, if you are interested in folklore, we can tell you a tale or two. If you are interested in facts, don't go looking for witches."

A witch's grave had been mentioned in at least four different books in connection with York, however, so I laughed with them and then turned around and studiously went about my task.

Up to my neck in the town's historical records, I had precious little time before the library closed. Throwing up my hands and trusting to intuition, I came upon the information in the first book I chose. There it was, the name of the witch buried in Old York Cemetery, Mary Jason. I ran across the street to the cemetery, where a stone with a huge boulder atop, supposedly locking her in for good, marked the spot.

Tingling with excitement, I approached the nearest grave with a big stone. There lay the body of a Revolutionary War hero, and nearby another large stone above another Patriot soldier. In the middle of the cemetery stood a tall monument, the only other massive stone in the place. It turned out to be a memorial for those killed in the great seventeenth-century Indian massacre. Mary had to be here. This was the oldest graveyard in town. My only recourse was to amble among the stones to see if I could find her family plot.

All by itself stood a strange memorial that looked like a stone bed, complete with headboard and footboard. It was not tall, but very sturdy, especially the middle stone that formed the "bed." The massiveness lay underground, not high in the air. There was Mary Jason's likeness etched in granite, a kindly, maternal image. The large eyes denoted clairvoyance, and the prominent breasts suggested mother of several children and/or sexual proclivity, generally associated with the Old Religion. This member of the Old Religion, another term for witchcraft, had a reason for steering clear. She wanted to make sure I had good intentions, of which I assured her with a small prayer.

As I knelt there at the grave, absorbing her personality through her epitaph, a heat emanated from the stone that warmed my hands and went halfway up my arms. Startled, a fearful thought flashed through my mind. What would she do next—rumble that stone and make herself appear?

(144)

While in this state of wonderment, I hadn't noticed a figure approaching from the left. He was a jolly sort, dressed in fisherman's clothes, who came over and talked to me about Mary. "So now you know who she is," he chuckled. It was the same villager who had joked with me before. Had he been watching me ever since I'd mentioned "witch's grave" to him?

Beneath the jokes lay a sense of responsibility and loyalty. He wasn't going to tell me anything until he was sure I meant no harm. "You seem to be a little shaken," he observed.

"Yes, yes, I am," was all I uttered.

He said, "Nothing to be afraid of. She's not on the black side; she's a white witch."

I was getting that impression. "People around here have been experiencing Mary ever since she died in 1774, 'far as I can tell."

Mary (Miller) Jason began her career at the age of twelve, when she cultivated an herb garden, according to her grandmother's instructions. The young witch would invite her friends over, and they'd play in the garden. Then Mary would explain each plant's purpose in healing. Sometimes she'd pluck a sprig or squeeze the oil from a flower, and rub it into a friend's scraped knee. The next day her friend would return without the wound.

The neighborhood parents became alerted to Mary's special herbs and powders. They allowed their children to play, but they kept a watchful eye on the Miller household. As a matter of fact, they kept an eye on Mary the rest of her twenty-nine-year-old life.

By the time Mary had become a parent, she had gone beyond the healing arts or "white magic" and made herself useful as an exorcist of sorts. This aspect of her career began with the old widow Wilcox's house. The widow was dead, and her cottage remained empty, except for one thing, an evil spirit. It was definitely a negative presence, and so viciously threatening that no one would sleep in the place or even approach its doorway. Eventually, the townspeople called upon Mrs. Jason to see what she could do. She took the job.

One evening, at dusk, Mary walked over to the haunted house, carrying a candle and her Bible. She bolted both doors, lit the candle, and began to read. Pretty soon the moon rose, and the following hours seemed to pass by in slow motion. Not a creak of wood nor an owl's hoot disturbed the peaceful night air. When Mary finished reading, she put down her book and upon inhaling discovered the foulest odor she'd ever encountered. Through the candlelight appeared a dark-hooded female figure of black but not Negroid skin. Her bulbous nose and long fingers pressed closer, but it was her eyes that were most formidable. In place of the normal eye structure burned two green rays of light. The figure reached out to envelop Mary, but the stouthearted lady stood up and shielded herself with white light. She cried, "Begone, thou servant of Satan!"

The evil thing's eyes flickered and went out, along with her malodorous presence. The rest of the night in the cottage remained calm, as well as the following nights.

In this century, Mary's fondness for children was apparent in the play area that used to be across from the cemetery. More than once a child went home telling his or her mother about "being pushed" on the swings when nobody else was around. Adults would also tell tales of "flowers that picked themselves" about dusk, by the graveyard's edge.

After the fisherman talked to me, the sun had just about spent its last orange rays on the old gravestones. I leaned over Mary's grave for a few parting words and got up to go. There to my right perched four shiny black crows, looking at one another and then at me, as if to say, "What is she doing here?" Mary's familiars, of course, sticking around to protect her. I stopped to look back—or was she one of them?

CHAPTER TWENTY-FOUR

PHANTOM OF THE OPERA HOUSE

T he Boothbay Harbor Opera House has had about everything in it but an opera. The impressive 1894 structure has housed minstrel shows, plays, town meetings, movies, talkies, basketball games—and a ghost.

Nobody knows who it is, but he lives on the second floor in a room that used to be the Knights of Pythias headquarters. The high courtroom ceiling bordered by heavy decorative plaster looks down upon a huge room built to let in plenty of sunlight. A grandfather clock, usually a towering piece, looks diminutive against the massive walls. At the opposite end of the room stands the only original article from the early Pythian days, an upright piano. The room reeks of ghostly energy; a happy, festive feeling floats about the dust-covered furniture.

Next door lies the adjacent art gallery, which takes up the rest of the floor. If it hadn't been for the director of the gallery, the memory of the ghost probably would have disintegrated with the cobwebs. Mr. Arthur Stanley relates his experience.

The year was 1977. Mr. Stanley of Philadelphia was looking around for a building suitable for a gallery, and he'd heard that the second floor of the Opera House was available. He fell in love with the place before he even opened the door. The late nineteenth-century architecture struck his fancy as he traveled up the staircase past the stained-glass windows. The front upstairs room was cluttered with old things, including a podium and rugged wooden benches draped with flags. Definitely a man's sort of place. Where dust now filtered the air, so did tobacco smoke many years ago.

Stanley's attention turned to the well-lit open space adjoining this room. A perfect setup for artwork, especially large sculpture. He was imagining where the pieces would go when he heard music coming from the direction of the front room. Thinking that it must have been coming from the street, he walked over and stood aghast at the sight before him. The piano keys were moving, but there was nobody playing the piano.

The rent was so reasonable (now he knew why) and the place so ideal, that Stanley went ahead with his plans, in spite of what he had seen. After the gallery's grand opening, he took time to look up the history of the Pythian room, in hopes of finding a clue to the "piano player."

It wasn't easy. The Pythian Knights were a secret society, many in number but few in talkers. There was no reason to divulge any information to the gallery operator, a man "from away." He had to dig on his own, and this he did wholeheartedly. Stanley wasn't sure he wanted a repeat performance of his first day, and if it happened again, in front of customers, what then? Would it drive away business or bring more in?

He found out through a Pythian wife visiting the gallery that the same incident had occurred after a Fourth of July party in 1957. Six hundred Knights had paraded, performed a drill, and acted out a pageant before they were able to relax and let loose at the evening ball. Their wives had had a long day, too, and were ready to party. They asked the orchestra to play an extra hour, and then people started milling their way toward the door.

Almost everyone had left, except for the wife in question and her husband. As they were nearing the exit, the woman heard piano music and thought that one of the musicians was goofing around after hours. All the musicians, however, were busy loading instruments into their vehicles. When she saw that the keys were moving with no one near the piano, she mentioned it to her husband. "Oh Clara," he said, "don't you know that's a player piano." She laughed as she remembered her foolishness.

Arthur cleared his throat and tried to correct her misconception. He said, "Clara, it is a regular piano with a player piano device attached, but the device is not automatic. In order for the keys to operate, a lever under the keyboard must be pulled, and the foot pedals must be pulled out from the bottom of the piano. Then someone has to pump the pedals!" The woman said nothing but her face turned white, and she left the room never once glancing back at the instrument she'd wondered at, twenty years ago.

It was shortly after Clara's visit that Benjamin Dunn, an elderly cafe dweller, told his cousin's story. "Cousin Edward doesn't talk of it much, but he'll never forget it." Arthur tried to remember Ben's exact words. "In November 1949, a grand celebration took place at the Opera House, to honor the thousandth inductee to the Knights of Pythias. Delegations from Bath, Lewiston, Livermore Falls, Portland, and Rumford attended the function. There was music and dancing till way into the night. Cousin was on 'clean-up committee,' so he was there with two other fellows after the rest had gone home. Edward was way up on a high ladder when he heard the piano playing from down below. He looked past the streamers of crepe paper over toward the stage, and there set that piano a goin' with nobody playing it. The other men saw it, too, and they all looked at one another. Well, they thought they were too tired to care about anything right then, but I tell you that woke 'em up some."

Asa White had been listening in on Ben's conversation in the coffee shop, not saying a word. When Ben was done, Asa, a real old-timer, spoke up. He said to Ben, "That party you spoke about might have been some good, but 'twas nothin' compared to the Two-Day Field Day the Knights held in the fall of 1907. The whole town was jam-packed. People from all over come in steamers for the parade, clambake, ball game, races, and fat man's dance. Yes sir, and did we ever have a piano player for that one. Earl Cliff was his name. Gawd, he was so good they called him 'Fingers' for short. 'Course, I was just a kid at the time, but I can see it just like it was yesterday."

Stanley realized he'd never know for sure who the phantom of the opera house represented. It could have been Earl; he seemed to do well at celebrations. Whoever it was he wanted to be remembered in the spirit of the music that played for so many good times at the old Opera House.

(154)

CHAPTER TWENTY-FIVE

BAT

Bat is my maternal grandmother. This chapter is dedicated to her, at the suggestion of my brother-in-law, who stood agape at hearing about all her intrusions during the period of my writing this book. She communicated not only to me, but also to my father, my brother, and my daughter.

Helen Ward Batastini died September 26, 1987, at her little cottage in Maine, called The Lone Maple. She was sick and wanted to die, but she did not want to be forgotten, as we all found out.

Her first manifestation was to my brother Lou. He had arrived with my dad in May 1988 for a week's stay at Fernwood cottage, my parents' house, just in front of my grandmother's. Dad was still in the car when Lou walked in the back entry. To his surprise, a potato flipped out of a basket on the shelf and rolled across the floor. Too tired to dwell upon it, he brought in all the luggage from

(155)

the car and took out his radio to listen to the Red Sox. He had just finished putting new batteries in it, when something caught his eye in the TV room. It turned out that Dad was getting the Red Sox game on TV. The two men watched the game without interruption until a deafening blast of music brought them back to the kitchen. Lou's radio dial had been turned to maximum volume. My brother put the potato incident with the radio incident and came up with one adjective: spooky. He went so far as to call my mother on the telephone and relate what had happened. She said, "Well, you know Grandma always hated potatoes (because they were fattening) and music (because she considered it the downfall of her son).

Dad just pooh-poohed the whole thing. He didn't believe in ghosts. Besides, it was "against the Catholic religion," according to him. (This argument I could never figure out, because in the old days the third Person of the Trinity included the Holy Ghost.) Even in 1976 when NBC came to the Fernwood house to do a documentary on psychic phenomena, Dad refused to witness the proceedings. "Oh, come on," was his standard response for ghostly tales. He never lost a night's sleep at Fernwood as opposed to my mother, who always kept three baseball bats under the bed. Don't ask me how the bats would have fended off a ghost.

Anyway, it was my dad who got Grandma's next dose of mischief. One night he went to bed early, over at The Lone Maple. He must have been asleep about an hour when a sudden chill awakened him. He shivered and drew the covers up to his chin, but what happened next gave him a greater chill. Something tugged at his blanket and made it land at the bottom of the bed. Tail wagging between his legs, Dad told Mom the whole story, but I never got wind of it until Mom inadvertently said something. "You knew I was writing this book on ghosts, and you weren't going to tell me?" I exclaimed to my father. He said, "Well, I didn't want to hear any 'I told you so's.'"

You might wonder how Helen came to be called "Bat." Primarily, "bat" is a symbol of watchfulness. Helen's first manifestation to me was the appearance of herself about twenty years younger than at her death. She was sitting at a window inside The Lone Maple, happily rocking and watching her great-grandchildren play on the porch.

Secondly, bats are clean, tidy animals equipped with excellent radar, and lacking in any desire to harm humans. That was Helen, fastidious, generous—and talk about radar. When we were kids, she knew what we were doing and where all the time without even being around. Of course, with a twinkle in her eye, she'd always tell us she was a witch.

The first time I walked into her house after her death, I was on a cleaning mission because my eldest son was going to stay there. I mentally heard her say, "It's about time somebody came over here to clean this place up. I knew it would be you, Carol."

The whole time I was there, I could feel her following me around, as if she were supervising the job.

(157)

Thirdly, Grandma's last name includes "Bat."

Lastly, at the Northport meeting where I met the two women who collaborated with me on the Sally Weir search, I had announced prior to the meeting that I felt my grandmother had led me there. And what do you think was flying around the rafters towards the end of the evening? A small brown bat.

Helen had a ready sense of humor, so I shouldn't have been surprised when she played a trick on me. I had brought downstairs from my room in Fernwood a bottle of Amaretto di Soronno to use in a birthday cake for Dad. I put it on the dining room table and plunk, it made a noise. I hoped no one had heard, because it was supposed to be a surprise. Then I went over to the kitchen to join everyone for supper. After supper I went to the dining room to get the liqueur, and there on the table was the paper bag in which I'd brought it down. Only thing, it was empty! I asked if anyone had seen the bottle. The answer was "No." Had anyone removed anything from the dining room table? "No."

I said, "This is crazy," and went about the house looking in the most stupid places. When I reached the top of the stairs, it dawned on me what had happened. "Okay, Grandma, please tell me where the Amaretto is. You know I can't make this cake without it. Please show me where you put it." I found myself walking down the hall and into the front bedroom. There it was, atop one of the bedspreads. I sensed her chuckling at me.

The final oddity to date was what sounded like

a bowling ball rolling down the upstairs Fernwood hallway and crashing into some glass at the end of its journey. My daughter, my brother, and I all heard it in the middle of the night. The next morning there was no evidence of either ball or broken glass.

. . . Is there an end to this chapter?

EPILOGUE: OUTTAKES

They both occurred on my journey to the west'ard. In the Ogunquit chapter I didn't mention that my search for a crystal led me to stop at this place that had gypsy pictures and astrological signs painted all over. Upon setting foot inside the door, I was accosted by a female voice croaking out of a very short body. The voice immediately started in on what sounded like a Garment District sales pitch. "Readings for five dollars, cards for ten, stones for twenty." She asked, "Where are you from?" I wanted to say, "You're supposed to tell me." She said, "How old are you, forty-five?" I was forty-one. She said, "When were you born—are you a Pisces?" I am a Capricorn. That did it. I beat it out of there before she started guessing my weight.

In passing through Saco, my mother and I saw yellow letters painted on a brown background: "Visit the Haunted House of Captain Isaac Cutler." Gee, we thought, what a break. Haunted houses aren't usually advertised like that. We were right. After we drove in the driveway and met a white-faced actor with a stiff-legged gait, bearing a fake sword, we realized that it was all part of the amusement park next door.